Homegrown

Stories from the Farm

To my parents, who took me to the farm.

Homegrown

Stories from the Farm

by

Evelyn Hoyt Frolking

with

Tod A. Frolking

The McDonald & Woodward Publishing Company
Granville, Ohio

The McDonald & Woodward Publishing Company
431 East College Street, Granville, Ohio 43023
www.mwpubco.com

Homegrown: Stories from the Farm

Text and photographs copyright © 2013 by
Evelyn Hoyt Frolking and Tod A. Frolking

All rights reserved.

Printed in the United States of America by
McNaughton & Gunn, Inc., Saline, Michigan,
on paper that meets the minimum requirements of
permanence for printed library materials.

First printing February 2013

10 9 8 7 6 5 4 3 2 1
20 19 18 17 16 15 14 13

Library of Congress Cataloging-in-Publication Data

Frolking, Evelyn Hoyt.
  Homegrown : stories from the farm / Evelyn Hoyt Frolking ; with
Tod A. Frolking.
    p. cm.
  Includes bibliographical references and index.
  ISBN 978-1-935778-22-6 (perfectbound : alk. paper)
  1. Agriculture—Ohio—Anecdotes. 2. Local foods—Ohio—
Anecdotes. I. Frolking, Tod A. (Tod Alexander) II. Title. III. Title:
Stories from the farm.
  S521.5.O3F76 2013
  635.09771—dc23

2012051276

Endorsements for

Homegrown
Stories from the Farm

In an era of increasing consumer interest and knowledge about their food choices, this book allows us to gaze back from the other side of the plate, to understand the challenges and passions that drive the local food movement from the producers' point of view.

— Carol Goland, Executive Director
Ohio Ecological Food & Farm Association
Columbus, OH

Homegrown *is an interesting book which chronicles the effort and challenges of six families who have dedicated themselves to producing quality locally grown food. Those who purchase local food and those who hope to grow clean healthy food whether in a home garden or for sale will find this book useful.*

— Gene Branstool
Farmer, former Ohio State Representative and Senator,
and Assistant Secretary of Agriculture
in the Clinton Administration
Utica, OH

As Evelyn Frolking suggests in her book, farmers markets are the star attractions in towns and cities across the nation, and Granville's is no exception. Homegrown *contains wonderful stories about relationships between small growers and local consumers that strengthen our neighborhoods and their economies.*

— Board of Directors
Granville Area Chamber of Commerce
Granville, OH

Table of Contents

Preface

When the Granville Area Chamber of Commerce first decided to sponsor a farmers market some 20 years ago, I was among those who stepped up to be a market master. My childhood on the farm seemed adequate qualification to interact with farmers and manage the details of a Saturday sale of food from local gardens. And, truthfully, now that I was a townie, I was eager to feel the breeze of a farmer's life again. The market was a small, quiet affair then. Card tables, truck beds, folding chairs: the set was simple. The food set out on those surfaces was fresh and varied: the morning's garden harvest. People drifted in. They socialized, bought a little food and came back week after week, strengthening friendships and likely their health. Since then, farmers markets have grown up and now they are star attractions in towns and cities across the nation. As the demand for fresh, clean food soars nationwide in the face of a food system we no longer quite trust, farming is respected again, even admired, emulated. After years away from a childhood on the farm, I wanted to hear what life was like now on the other side of the market table.

My interest in food is rooted in my family and my daily life. My mother is German and she grew up in the family bakery in German Village in Columbus, Ohio's capital city. At age 90, she still makes the best apple pie in town. Our son, a young college graduate with a successful new job in environmental geology, came home one day and told us he wanted to go to culinary school. Today, he is a passionate chef, living and working in Oregon, a state known and respected for culinary progressiveness and fine fresh food. When I was offered a position to teach essay writing at Denison University, the college on the hill in Granville, the content was mine to choose. I chose food, specifically, the issues surrounding the food industry that so increasingly unsettled me and were virtually unrecognized by my young students.

My husband, Tod Frolking, a professor at the college in the Geoscience Department, is a soil scientist and geographer. We talk a lot about food, where it comes from, what has been done to it and to the land, and the trajectory the country has been on. We travel frequently and the food is always something we enjoy and take note of as we walk among the locals in their markets. Tod has written several parts of this book, using his experience and knowledge to add insights and background. Without his contributions and his counsel, I believe the book would be less worthy and my deepest gratitude goes to him for his participation, encouragement, and support over the long months of writing, teaching my class, and conducting the small business I own and operate on the side.

Thanks also to photographer and friend Gary Chisolm, who traveled twisting country roads and long highways with me to let you see the farmers, face to face, and who became as taken by their stories as I was. And thanks, too, to the Harvey family for sharing a photo of their daughter, Erin, standing in her sunflower patch. Lastly, without the interest and support of Jerry McDonald of McDonald & Woodward Publishing Company and his marketing manager, Trish Newcomb, the book would likely still be on my computer. Their guidance and advice has been invaluable.

And finally, and most appreciatively, I want to thank the families who sat with me at their kitchen tables, walked the fields, poked through the greenhouses, and told me their stories. It has been my honor to acknowledge and affirm them for the hard work they do from early mornings to late evenings, alone as they are in those moments on the land.

> *This hour in history needs a dedicated circle of transformed nonconformists. The saving of our world from pending doom will come not from the action of a conforming majority but from the creative maladjustment of a dedicated minority.*
>
> — Martin Luther King, Jr.
> *Strength to Love,* 1963

Homegrown

Stories from the Farm

On Farming

*Many of us who aren't farmers or gardeners still have some
element of farm nostalgia in our family past, real or imagined:
a secret longing for some connection to a life where a rooster
crows in the yard.*

> — Barbara Kingsolver
> *Animal, Vegetable, Miracle*, 2007

Clara was legally blind from birth, her farm life days of
colorless shadows. Her husband, Bill, suffered a degenerative
eye disease that left him struggling to make sense of the ghost-
like world his dairy herd had become. Together this middle-
aged couple had spent a lifetime beating the odds and making
the most of their 120-acre farm just outside of Granville, Ohio.
It was time for them to leave their farming life behind and, although I really knew them only as a child knows that one family
is leaving a place and another is coming, I felt their loss. The herd
was sold, the farm equipment auctioned, and the little farmhouse
with dark, oddly colored walls and a well scrubbed plainness gave
way to my family as we moved from the rural suburbs of Columbus to the country with our band of horses, dogs, and cats.

◀ As we stroll down the farm lane, Warren Taylor of Snowville Creamery
tells me about the farmers who provide grass-grazed milk for his dairy.

3

Food that we now distinguish as "real food" was growing in our new farm neighborhood at that time. It was flavorful to be sure and I now know it was also clean and nutritious, grown free of synthetic inputs by our neighbors and their neighbors in this farming community. It was just matter of fact. Today, if we're paying attention, we are witnessing the American public gradually reacquaint themselves with what they eat as they turn away from mass produced monocultures that sustain the fast food industry and the over processed products that fill the innards of grocery stores, a food system that has become just matter of fact for them, too. And, if we're paying attention, we're witnessing a whole new generation discover their local food — fresh from the field, rich tasting vegetables, milk, and meats the way they used to be and cheese soft and fragrant, all produced by farmers who can tell them how it was grown or produced. They will find vegetables grown free of synthetic pesticides and fertilizers in soils these farmers nurture through ecologically sound methods. Likely, they will also find meats and dairy products from livestock raised on grassy pastures without added hormones and antibiotics added to their diet. And this food will travel a few miles to the dinner table, not hundreds. Whether concerns for the environment and its dwindling resources, compassion for the welfare of animals, health reasons, or all of these combined, the public is tuned into what they are putting into their bodies like never before. In 2007, the New Oxford American Dictionary named "locavore" the word of the year to describe those who eat only food grown within a 100-mile radius of their home.

Behind the scenes of this changing culture is a small and growing army of men and women, clusters of producers who are driving this food movement from the farms and fields of our countryside. Some are not only young but new, a generation defined by intentions. From all walks of life, they have stepped onto the land to become growers, bent on enhancing the economic, environmental, and social health of their communities, themselves and the larger society. This "organic generation" bolsters an earlier generation of men and women who sensed early on that something was amiss on the land. Disregarding popular and to them unnatural practices that transformed farming over the last 50 years into chemical laden mega farms, they have continued to grow food in clean healthy ways, their search for food sovereignty largely under the public radar. On these pages, farmers tell their stories about their work, their lifestyles, and their collaborative efforts to build more locally based, self-reliant food economies where local is as much about trust and relationships as it is about farming. They recognize with pleasure, relief, and excitement, that they are caught up in, even steering, what seems to be a cosmic shift in how farming is practiced. And in the simplest of terms, their stories tell us about carrots, cows, cheese, and milk.

All over the country, grassroots local food movements are beginning at home. Around my small town and all across Ohio and the nation, communities like mine are experiencing something extraordinary. Backyard gardens and farm fields are exploding with jam-packed rows of red and green lettuce, tomatoes, beets, chard, and carrots, vegetables of all sorts, abundant in varieties never found in grocery stores. A drive down a county road near my home finds former fields of corn and soybeans now quilted in textured mosaics, palettes of color — yellow beets, red lettuce, purple eggplant. Funny, it's such a strange, but warming, sight.

Granville, founded in 1805, sits near the center of the state, a neighbor to Ohio's capital city of Columbus. A township of 13,300 acres and 4,500 residents surrounds a village of 3,500. This small village, packed with well-kept 19th Century houses, many of which are listed on the National Register of Historic Places, resides in Licking County, the state's second largest, a county named after the salt licks that became a natural resource for native people and early settlers. A liberal arts college founded in 1831, Denison University sits on the hill overlooking the village, adding two thousand or so students to its population during the academic year. The area is a beehive of food interest. The Saturday farmers market swarms with small-scale farmers and eager backyard gardeners ready to talk about what they grow and how they grew it as you fill your bags full. Standing behind tables filled with pyramids of tomatoes, stacks of beets, or buckets of rainbow chard, young ordinary people who have a knack and passion for growing things are alongside long tenured farmers who relish a limelight they can hardly have imagined after years of public apathy towards the vegetables they grow or the livestock they raise.

History offers a bit of insight into this new popularity in farming now when large scale, highly mechanized agriculture sees diminishing returns. Change happens gradually in most things, but post wartime research in the mid-20th Century gave farmers a quick and powerful arsenal of pesticides and super-fertilizers that allowed them to increase production exponentially. As the nation's highway systems expanded coast to coast, the fast food industry populated roadways, coming to dominate agriculture and the diet of the American public so quickly that they now control much of what we grow in this country. The Reagan administration in the 1980s, wanting to increase exports, further pushed agriculture into a large scale mass production model with policies that increased subsidies for planting commodity crops, corn and soybeans mostly, fence row to fence row. And with their new chemical inputs and mechanized production methods, farmers could do it. Multi-national corporations increasingly turned agriculture into an agribusiness of monocultures to control the country's meat, grain, dairy, and egg supply. We took it in stride. Common sense all but disappeared. Butcher shops, green grocers, and roadside markets morphed into grocery stores, supermarkets, and big box stores, all increasingly bloated with over processed food. The term, "edible food-like substance," came into being. As long as we had money, food, or something like it, was available and it was cheaper and cheaper. As farming to meet a market largely driven by fast food and corn to feed livestock took over Ohio fields then, the sight today of vegetables growing on plots of land formerly dominated by endless acres of corn and soybeans is even more remarkable.

After decades of passive consuming, we are beginning to find out how our food is handled and produced. Often it's not pretty and as we learn more about the American diet, we're starting to understand that it's not that healthy either, for us, the animals, or for the planet. For the first time in 50 years, children are expected to live shorter lives than their parents. Widespread food poisoning from bad peanut butter, tainted ingredients in children's formula, e-coli in meat, and illnesses or deaths caused by contaminated spinach grab our attention. What we eat, where it comes from, who is growing it, and how far it travels have become vocal questions in a country where people now realize that what they eat can make them and the earth sick. And all the while we've been dismantling our concept of food, we've been unwittingly doing the same to our bodies. Type two diabetes, heart conditions, and obesity head the list of diet-related health consequences, now in epidemic proportions. In 2030, half of the adult American population is predicted to be obese.

My family didn't realize the value of our new rural life in the 1960s, the years when farming was beginning to undergo some of its most eruptive changes. In those early days, we busied ourselves with renovating and restoring buildings and land that had gently, lovingly slipped into decline. We repainted, repaired, mowed, and moved in. We planted a garden. My younger sister and I were delirious with excitement at the prospect of exploring pastures, cornfields, woods, and streams. How could we ever discover the many mysteries hidden in a shaggy fencerow, a bottomless pool in the rocky stream, a towering boulder adrift, perched alone on a mound of earth? How did it get there, we wondered?

Our farm was surrounded on all sides by farms like it, most between 100 and 200 acres. On ours, like most in the early part of that decade, a two-story timber frame barn found animals living downstairs and hay filling the mow upstairs. A towering cement silo, its silvery dome long gone, was a castle turret to us as we twisted our heads through the small window-like openings at the base to look for blue sky high above. Inside, an aging mattress of dried darkened silage — remnants of a slurry of fermenting grasses — and pale stringy weeds seeking the distant light blanketed the circular floor, reminders of the dairy farm we replaced. Over time, as Bill's farm needed more space for his herd, a long linear metal pole barn was attached to the wooden barn. It was there we were certain our horses would now live like kings.

Our farmer neighbors on all sides were long on the land. These kindly plainspoken folks of the Browns' generation made their living milking cows, raising chickens, or running beef cattle, sometimes right through our fences to our citified horror and dismay. I was often reminded that we weren't real farmers like they were and early admiration for their stamina and knowing took hold as we settled into country life. Instead of planting crops and raising livestock, my parents, who both worked day jobs, rented out swaths of our land for others to plant or make hay on shares, while taking equally sizable fields out of production as part of a popular federal program at the time, a program created to uphold the price of agricultural goods by lessening supply. On those chunks of fertile soil, we agreed to not plant one seed of the common commodity crops, corn and soybeans, that others covered their land with, in return for cash payments. Occasionally, we had a handful of sheep or cattle or chickens or goats as well, but these gentle farm animals were mostly 4-H projects, animals from which we learned lessons of life.

It was during those farm years that I came to appreciate our neighbors for the lifestyle they had chosen and the food they provided us. I saw them raise blisters on their hands, earn a forever farmer's tan, and leave their houses unpainted for yet another year in order to buy a hay baler or replace a tractor. Through their life on the land, they were growing or raising local food, some of it our food. From Wib we got fresh milk in the early mornings, still warmly fragrant when my father brought it home in glass half-gallon bottles. From Charley and Hazel, I ate my first brown egg.

These farms are gone now, some broken apart into building lots, some divided and gobbled up by new highways, others consolidated into long acres of corn and soybeans. In the years between 1959 and 1997, the number of farms in Licking County halved. That trend continues. Today, consolidation and exurban sprawl, the increasing value of farmland, and an aging conventional farming community finds few small farms left. Remaining farmers, now mostly in their 60's, who adjusted and stayed continue to plant many hundreds of acres of subsidized commodity crops, the only way to make a living now. Ohio ranks 14th of 50 states in subsidies, receiving $69.2 million for commodity subsidies where just 10% of farms collect 77% of all subsidies. One farmer friend in the county is typical. He owns 260 acres, but farms over 2,000 in genetically modified (GMO) corn and soybeans with seeds and chemical inputs coming from Monsanto, a mega corporation that controls every move conventional farmers make in this country. He owns barnfuls of tractors and big machinery to grow the vast fields of subsidized commodity crops. We are planting, planting, planting, but little of it is real food for Ohioans.

The changes in how people are reacting to their food sources may be most telling from the excitement of the elbow to elbow street setting in Granville where the Saturday farmers market runs May through October. Saturday has become market day across the country with mid-week and year round markets increasing to round out direct sales of local food. They are fun, social events, candy stores full of real foods. In 2011, the United States Department of Agriculture (USDA) reports 1,000 new farmers markets opened in the U.S., bringing the total to 7,175, a whopping 17% increase from the previous year. In 1994, the year record keeping began for this method of food marketing, 1,755 farmers markets operated. In Ohio alone, the number of farmers markets in 2011 increased 31% with 278 operating in cities and in small towns like Granville. Food co-ops, food hubs, community gardens, and Community Supported Agricultural arrangements (CSAs), add to the mix of broadening local food distribution. The most recent data collected in 2007 by the USDA on CSAs nationwide, for example, show 12,549 farms market their produce through these farm investment arrangements with customers. This stunning growth in the supply and demand chain for local foods could only happen because dotted here and there on small plots of land all across the state and the country people are growing food again.

Homegrown celebrates this trend by sharing the motivations and contributions of six Ohio families who are committed

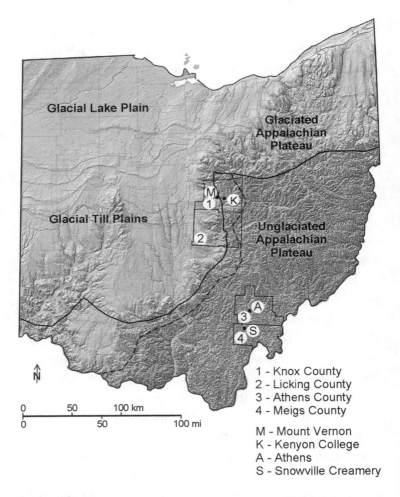

Shaded relief map of Ohio showing counties and other locations discussed in the text. Note that Snowville Creamery (Chapter 6) is in Meigs County. The solid line approximates the southern limit of the late-Wisconsinan glacial advance, and the dashed line reflects the furthest advances of earlier ice sheets. The base map is from http://nationalatlas.gov/mapmaker.

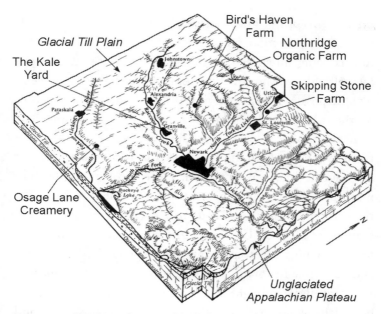

Diagram of Licking County, Ohio, showing generalized topography and geology. Five of the farm locations discussed in the book (Chapters 1-5) and key towns and cities in the county are indicated. The diagram is from Parkinson et al., 1992.

to growing and preparing clean healthy foods for local consumption. Here we devote a chapter to each of these six families, five of which are clustered geographically in central Ohio to supply their local markets. The sixth stands as a model for the possibilities of widening the distribution of healthy, quality products in an expanding local-food culture. Through their words and actions, they reveal why and how they do what they do.

So while neither Granville nor Ohio is particularly unique in this nationwide movement, the town and the state are microcosms of this grassroots wave, one in which sustainable local food production, processing, distribution, and consumption is being integrated to enhance the economic, environmental, and social health of the community. Right now, it seems like the possibilities are tangible. These farmers, those people on the other side of the market table, tell their stories here from the producer level. Most, like farmers before them, are family ventures. Farming is revisited in this modern era, for sure, and technology, education, and environmental realities make it sort of a whole new ball game. Interspersed within their stories, my husband, Tod Frolking, a geographer and soil scientist at Denison University, and who walks with me close to the ground, adds insights into Ohio's geologic, agricultural, and economic history as they apply to the work of farmers.

I've always thought that the lives of ordinary people can be equally as fascinating as those who have gained fame and fortune. The farmers in this book, largely unseen and unrecognized in the world, are representative of that source. I've come to know them all. As you'll see, they face obstacles head on, recognize windows of opportunity in a changing culture, and find creative solutions to persistently push forward. Like others across the country, at their core, they want to better the food environment through sovereignty, foster community around food, protect the land and its resources, make a living wage, and live the lifestyle of their choice by putting their hands gently in the soil or lightly on the animals. Homegrown as they are, these ordinary people may be quietly saving us all.

Chapter 1

Starting Up

The single greatest lesson the garden teaches is that our relationship to the planet need not be zero-sum, and that as long as the sun still shines and people still can plan and plant, think and do, we can, if we bother to try, find ways to provide for ourselves without diminishing the world.

— Michael Pollan
The Omnivore's Dilemma:
A Natural History of Four Meals, 2006

She is almost indistinguishable, a distant movement on a plot of freshly turned soil stretching nearly half an acre against her lean hundred pounds the only clue to her presence. As I approach, I see the slender young woman take long, even steps down a long row sifting seeds from a paper cone into the furrowed planting bed, a bed she had carved from the plowed expanse with a hoe and shovel. She stops briefly to survey her work, adjust her broad-brimmed straw hat against the sun, and continue to the end. A few more trips back and forth and the rainbow carrot seeds will be in the ground.

Later, she begins a series of walks to a nearby stream that flows parallel to the newly cultivated garden. As diminutive as

Erin Harvey of The Kale Yard amidst her garden containing five different kinds of kale along with many other greens and vegetables destined for sale at the Granville Farmers Market.

17

she is in size, watering 50-foot rows of newly planted seeds with a green plastic watering can seems a gigantic and unseemly task. She is working with the property owner to engineer a gravity flow system that will bring water from its source 400 feet away to a round holding tank at the head of her garden. A perennial current appears from a storm sewer under the road, its spring-fed source on the hillside beyond. But that's not yet in place. If it works at all, other challenges lay ahead. How to get enough head for a strong flow, how to lead the water to the 300-gallon plastic tank she hauled down to the garden site, and then how to get the water to the planting beds. Lots of questions. Much to ponder. So for now, she carries the plastic can, back and forth, for as long as it takes to moisten the new seeds and settle them into the soil.

Before she calls it a day, she tries out an idea she has been turning over in her head. Carrots germinate slowly, she knows. Weeds grow, well, like weeds. From a pile of flattened cardboard boxes she has collected, she covers the rows of newly planted seeds with the odd-shaped pieces and anchors them with rocks. She hopes to retain precious moisture and deter weed growth in the coming weeks as the seeds slowly germinate. It seems unlikely to plant seeds and then plaster them over, she knows, but she thinks this strategy may create the window of time needed to let the thin feathery carrot shoots push up against their ceiling of cardboard unimpeded. Especially so, she thinks, in a new garden space where densely rooted pasture grass has ruled the land for untold years until a week ago when she turned the soil. Clearly, those grasses are quick to reclaim the space at first chance and, in fact, are already starting to do so as she stands back and looks across her garden and down the bordering fence she erected as deer protection.

Thirty-year-old Erin Harvey is a small-scale vegetable farmer, one of a new breed who has stepped onto the land to fulfill a need in her life and to share the bounty of her garden with those around her. She is starting a market garden on this sunny spot of land in Granville. When she's not planting, transplanting, hoeing, watering, or harvesting, she works a part-time job. She is like thousands of young, college educated people across the country poised to redefine the American culture along with its diet. Growing up in a green generation, an organic generation, where Earth Day, recycling, and healthy real food took root in her heart, she and others like her grow food naturally without synthetic pesticides and herbicides. They want to know where their food comes from. They want others to know, too. They have learned that chemical aids to increasing production have been overused and abused, causing untold problems for the land and its people alike. And like many of her breed, they are practical and realistic. Mostly from cities or suburbs, they often don't own land, and they are intentionally choosing the soil over an office, knowing they might be charting this course in their life at their own financial peril.

The National Young Farmers' Coalition surveyed more than a thousand young farmers about their biggest challenges. "Lack of capital" and "land access" ranked high, higher than health care, finding profitable markets, and lack of marketing skills. Seventy-eight percent of the 1,300 respondents also reported they did not grow up on family farms. The majority of the respondents were women in their late twenties and early thirties, just like Erin. In Erin's world and among those in a new generation like her, growing food for themselves and their community is as natural as breathing. The 2007 agricultural census reports that more that one-quarter of all farmers are age 65 or older and the average age is 57. Over the past century, the total number of American farmers has declined – from over 6 million in 1910 to just over 2 million today. For each farmer under 35 there are now 6 over 65. The USDA expects that one-quarter (500,000) of all farmers will retire in the next twenty years. And the vast majority of these farmers are conventional farmers working in a subsidized commodity environment. It's not clear yet how many young farmers like Erin there are across the country, but one measure is the number of farmers markets where they often make their first public foray into selling what they grow. For now, they produce a sliver of food, but in Ohio, with the National Farmers Markets Directory documenting the rise of markets in double digit growth, it's fair to say we're well into a social movement they are driving.

In 1999, Erin left her hometown of Lancaster, Ohio, about 25 miles from Granville, to attend Earlham College in Richmond, Indiana, a Quaker college with strong values towards the earth and social well being. She became a peace and global studies major. The idea of gardening to produce food for others was the furthest thing from her mind then.

"My father is a big gardener," she said. "He used to take me to garden centers where I'd sit under benches of plants and wait for him. He is a teacher and I spent the summers with him in the garden planting peas. And then I got over it. I didn't care at all about the garden. I went to college and if you said I was going to be a farmer, I would have laughed out loud at you."

It didn't take long for Erin to become interested in food issues though. She began to see the problems surrounding food as social justice issues presented through her course studies. "That's kind of how I got hooked," she said. "One of my first classes was a philosophy class called Food Ethics that took the angle of food issues. It really grounded things for me."

She remembers other markers in her shift towards growing food. Frances Moore Lappé, author of *Diet for a Small Planet*, a seminal book on global hunger that puts forward the thesis that worldwide hunger is not for the lack of food, but for the lack of political will, visited the campus. "She helped me understand that the problem is not that we don't have enough food to feed people. We produce tons of food. Lack of good food is a social problem."

"If I want to be a small organic farmer right now in my life, I am able to sell my vegetables at the Granville Farmers Market to an upscale crowd who can buy them, but I think about access and the right to grow what I want a lot."

She sees other states like Vermont and Maine as models when she talks about food sovereignty, growing what she wants under her own ethical standards. These states have organized, written mission statements, and taken action on local levels. In Vermont, for example, the Vermont Coalition for Food Sovereignty is a grassroots coalition of people from diverse political, religious, and socioeconomic backgrounds. In 2010, they drafted a resolution that individual towns in the state are beginning to adopt. Barre, Vermont, for example, became the second town to pass the measure supporting food sovereignty. "The Resolution asserts that the people have the right and responsibility, individually and through their elected officials, to resist any and all infringements on the rights to save seed, grow, process, consume and exchange food and farm products within the State of Vermont. The statement is intended to catalyze and inspire a conversation among all of the people in Vermont about food freedom and security in a time of global unrest and to stand as a template and measure by which all food and agricultural policy in the State of Vermont should be held against," the Coalition declares.

Food sovereignty, the right to grow and sell food largely unrestricted by government influence, is on the lips of local farmers and food producers like Erin. It's part of what they aspire to when they talk the long view. They value organic production, but shudder at the growing list of standards necessary to obtain USDA certification. Erin participates in these conversations with other young farmers at her local level and calls upon her experiences during and after college as evidence that sovereignty over food is a worthy issue and that it can coexist alongside organic, or better yet, be intrinsic to it. Like some others who tell their stories on these pages, she sits on the Licking County Foods Council, a group formed about two years ago to forward and support a local food economy. She is also active in other groups where she can share her voice and listen to theirs.

"Local," like other words in the vocabulary of this food movement, is a moving target in definition. For some, food that is local is easily defined by distance: 50 miles from home is local, 100 miles is local, or a day's drive is considered local. In other ways, it's less precise and suggests broader implications. Does it have political connotations; does it imply a push back on globalization? Is it a marker of cultural change where bigger is really not better? Regardless, like "organic," "grass grazed," and "free range," it's part of the food language of the day. For Erin, it's simple. She lives and works in a town where she grows food and sells it to people who live there, too. People who value its honesty. Erin's conscientious entrepreneurship is well respected by her customers and her friends, and the qualities of her work are reflected in the vegetables she grows and takes to market. The broader implications are not lost on her by any means, but she takes it one step at a time, locally.

The summer after her first year at Earlham she interned with community food initiatives in Athens, Ohio, a progressive college town long supported by a rural food community of small farmers. "They have lots of community gardening programs so I helped out," she said. Then she found herself writing college papers focusing on food issues where she could. Her senior thesis on Local Food Systems and Environmental Justice received department honors.

She worked on the college's student farm, which "kind of ebbed and flowed," she said. In her senior year, she started a CSA project there and stayed through the summer after graduation to help manage its growth. She had by now spent summers working with organic farmers and learning hands on what it takes to grow food that is fresh, healthy, and free of pesticides and herbicides. "That's where I really learned about farming," she said. "That stuff has stuck with me, things I learned there I still go back to. One farmer in particular mentored me. Even though I have done other things since, I always come back to what she taught me."

Erin began to imagine herself in a rural farm setting, but at loose ends after graduation and wanting to maintain relationships she had developed, she moved to Philadelphia with her group of friends. "It was our goal to have some kind of a community after leaving college," she said. "We wanted to stay connected." She laughed and said they chose Philadelphia, an unlikely setting to begin a rural life, because she hoped they could all find jobs. "We hoped the Quakers would give us jobs," she grinned.

Erin sought out work in the non-profit world with hopes it would lead to full time work with a living wage and benefits, a chance to fulfill expectations she thought her society held for her and that her educated parents had modeled. She worked for AmeriCorps and then at a state-to-state food cupboard. Neither led to better paying work and when the opportunity to run an urban farm arose, she jumped at the chance. She was there for three years. "I realized the part I enjoyed the most was the actual growing of food," she said.

Perhaps it was then that her trajectory to a farming lifestyle began to take shape. After five years in Philly and a growing level of discontent with the non-profit world she had entered, Erin took what she believes was the first real step. "I thought if I really wanted to become a grower, I needed to learn more. I learned how to farm in an educational environment and I learned to grow informally by doing it, but I wanted to do something for myself that would focus on learning farming as a business," she said.

She had heard about a six-month apprenticeship program in ecological horticulture at the University of California at Santa Cruz. The program, founded in 1967, blends hands on experiential work with academic study in soil management, pest control, crop planning, irrigation, and other areas for those who may want to begin their own organic commercial farms or markets. Although the climate and crops grown differed from the Midwest (Erin admits she perhaps should have studied closer to home soil) she loved the experience. "It was a turning point for me," she said.

While there, Erin met a young woman from Alexandria, a small community just west of Granville, whose family-owned greenhouse business is well known in the county. That they both arrived on the other side of the country at the same time was enough to make them quick friends.

After the course and with the non-profit world behind her, for the time being at least, Erin returned to the east to work as an orchard assistant in Pennsylvania. "At Santa Cruz, I learned the material, but not how to apply it here. At the orchard, I learned how to actually run a farm in this part of the country. Their good management and good growing practices really influenced how I want to work now."

The market garden she tends this year is her second. After Santa Cruz and her stint at the orchard – where she decided she didn't want to grow fruit – she reunited with her local friend. Together, they began their first market garden. "We were both starting to feel like it was time to do this," she said. "I had this abstract idea of wanting to move home. I knew it would be cheaper if I wanted to buy land. I'd have the support system of my parents and their community. Everywhere I had lived never really felt like home. There is something about Ohio that I feel like even if I had been gone for ten years, I can say I'm from Lancaster and that has meaning."

Erin sees Ohio's agricultural scene for small-scale organics positively. With so much demand for local food and mounting concerns about conventional farming, she feels like she's getting in on the ground floor. It's beyond organic for her, though. Good growing practices and keeping food distribution on a local level, for her right now, trumps the trendy image of organic. Stiff restrictions make organic certification a daunting undertaking, one that will certainly require her to own her own land. Demand for good honestly produced local food is high and steady — albeit still in geographic pockets statewide — good Ohio soil and her network of friends and family give her the comfort and opportunity to experiment. "I'm using good growing practices," she said. "Ten years ago I wrote my thesis on growing good local food and how that was more important to people than being certified organic," she said. "It surprises me in some ways that today I'm part of a group of good hard working families who just want to grow good food in their own way."

Her first market garden struggled. Drenching rains until June delayed planting. Deer took a share of the garden despite a hastily erected fence. "I learned so much that first year," she said. "It was the first time I was making the decisions. I didn't always have the confidence. I got over that when the deer took the fence down." That first year became one of the wettest planting seasons in recent history and by the time they could finally harvest, it was August and her time at the farmers market was halved. Adding to that, her partnership with her friend ebbed. "We just discovered we didn't want to farm in the same way."

As winter set in, Erin found herself unemployed and uncertain about a future market garden. "It hit me that winter that if I don't make this happen, it will be the first time in nine years that I'm not on a farm. I can't let that happen."

Her new garden space, about one-half acre, sits on a six-acre property, an unusually large plot of "rural" land to be within village limits. From that acreage and with the support of the property owner, she carved out a rectangle that she cultivated, soil tested, fenced, and gradually planted. Her agreement with the property owner, who happily accepts vegetables as payment, allows her to farm the land for up to three years and maybe longer, giving her time to perhaps find land she can truly call her own. She found her breathing room.

The new garden sits adjacent to a popular Rail to Trails path that runs along the south side of the village. "That people are passing by feels good. I don't want to farm in isolation and I don't know if I just want to be a production farmer. It's not enough I think. I want this other piece of working the land with people who do what I do and value local food. I want it to be more social."

The spring-fed channel bordering the west side of the property trickles along as it has for years, but now also fills her water tank as the gravity flow project proved successful, surprising everyone with a two-to-four-gallons-per-minute

Erin's towering wall of blooming sunflowers borders the southern edge of her market garden and delights passers-by on the Granville bike path.

flow. A solar powered pump on the tank pushes the water through a hose with some added pressure, making watering easier now. A friend lent her a tiller to tackle the grass that quickly grew back. Her father visits some weekends to give her a hand, but for the most part, she gardens by herself, visiting daily to weed, water, pick flea beetles, look for groundhog intrusions, and do other chores of maintaining a garden. On one weekend she and her parents planted 250 tomato plants by hand to join the lettuce, fennel, peas, beets, and kale and other vegetables already growing.

In the unplanted space, the final quarter of the garden, Erin will plant the Three Sisters, the "holy trinity" of cooperative growth that provided a balanced diet for earlier generations. Corn, beans, and squash live efficiently together in mounds providing each other with physical protection and nutritional support. As the Indian corn and popcorn varieties she selected grow tall, they will provide a scaffold for her beans to vine and turn, twisting upwards as they seek the sun. At ground level, squash and melons cover the soil with dense vines, preserving moisture and blocking weed growth. Their prickly stems act as a defense to pests like groundhogs (they can be seen frolicking in the fields at dusk) who might be tempted to tunnel under the fence for a bite or two or three, as any farmer knows.

The wisdom of this style of planting continues below ground level. The beans are legumes, whose root nodules house bacteria that produce valuable ammonia from nitrogen in the air. Simply, as the bean plants peak and then break down, the soil is gradually enriched and supplies nitrates demanded by the hungry corn and squash. Eventually, all becomes compost to enrich the soil for next year's crops. Modern industrial corn farming, for example, requires heavy doses of nitrogen fertilizer to replace the nitrogen removed when the corn is harvested and when rainwater drains through the soil, leaving fields starkly barren over the winter. The Three Sisters, while not providing the super high yields of modern varieties of densely planted GMO corn, gives sustainable yields with little nitrogen loss. Further, the Three Sisters is a marvel to look at as it grows into artistic towers across the field.

Three weeks have passed. Erin removes the cardboard over the long rows deep in the garden. The carrots have sprouted.

Sidebar 1

Life of the Soil

Soil is the link between Earth's rocks and sediment and life concentrated on its surface. A gram (quarter teaspoon) of rich soil may host a billion bacteria, a million fungi, and a tremendous range of other life from yeast and algae to roundworms and rotifers. These power the decomposition of life's remnants and recycle nutrients so essential to new life. As organic material breaks down, resistant compounds and inaccessible materials remain as soil humus. Humus gives topsoil its dark color and promotes both water holding and nutrient exchange. A soil's fertility, that is its ability to provide essential nutrients to plants or crops, is directly linked to its humus content — often measured as organic carbon content, about 40% of soil organic matter is the element carbon.

Farmers have soils tested for nutrient availability and supplement their fields with the major nutrients nitrogen, phosphorous, and potassium, and with an array of minor and trace elements to insure healthy crop growth. The soil biochemical environment is exceedingly complex and soil analysis is necessarily reductionist, using various analytic methods to isolate specific elements or compounds. Rather than viewing the soil simply as a provider of essential nutrients, many agronomists, soil scientists, ecologists, and farmers now think more holistically about *soil health*, a concept that includes the quantity and distribution of organic matter as well as the numbers and diversity of soil micro and macro organisms. In many ways soil health is a pragmatic concept that can be observed by the health of plants, crop yields, and the quality of nearby streams and ground water.

Beyond its importance in soil fertility, soil carbon is drawing tremendous attention because of its relationship to the anthropogenic CO_2 budget and hence global climate change. Worldwide, soils are a major carbon reservoir, potentially storing 3–5 times as much carbon as all terrestrial above-ground plants and animals. In the 1800s, as European settlement spread westward into the Midwest and land was put under the plow, there would have been a large carbon flux as soil organic carbon was oxidized to atmospheric CO_2. Plowing overturns the soil and directly exposes soil organic matter to oxygen. Somewhat analogous to fanning the flames of a fire, soil microbial respiration would have accelerated, consuming soil organic matter. Climatologist William Ruddiman argues that human impact on atmospheric CO_2 began with development of agriculture 8,000 years ago, a trend that has continued as more and more land has been cultivated. Noted Ohio State University soil scientist Rattan Lal estimates that midwestern soils have lost 30–50% of their pre-settlement organic carbon.

This loss can be reversed, at least in the short term, with shifts from conventional to conservation tillage and with increased use of offseason cover crops. Both of these practices are now widely promoted. The net gain in soil carbon is even greater when converting plowed land to permanent hay or pasture and when animal or green manure is added to the field.

One of the stories in this book is about Snowville Creamery in southeastern Ohio. Pasturelands at Snowville, for example, have shown improved pasture quality with higher dairy yields as the health of the soil has been restored. As soil carbon levels increase, so too does the availability of soil nitrogen and other critical nutrients. With more organic matter in the soil, the structure and water holding capacity of the soil also increases. This further benefits plant growth, which then facilitates the incorporation of more organics into the soil. An additional benefit of soil health is disease resistance. Numerous recent studies indicate that a large diverse population of soil organisms can stabilize some plant pest populations preventing serious blights and thus reducing pesticide needs. Ecologists and economists now use the term *ecosystem services* to account for the myriad ways in which healthy ecosystems support the human endeavor. Healthy soils are central to this service.

— *Tod Frolking*

Chapter 2

Adjusting

There are two spiritual dangers in not owning a farm. One is the danger of supposing that breakfast comes from the grocery store, and the other that heat comes from the furnace.

— Aldo Leopold
A Sand County Almanac, 1949

The icy wind hurries us through the doorway that leads into the long, hooped building. As we pile into the warm barn, a staccato choir of shrill bleating voices greets us, the warmth of the place fragrant with the soft earthy scents of hay, grain, milk, and goat. We might have a treat in our pockets or we might just like to give a stroke or two to the long line of wide-eyed faces stretching over the fence, long necked and lined up like soldiers at attention. With nearly a hundred nannies and kids in the barn, every hopeful goat eye is trained on us, visitors to their performance.

It is early spring. A handful of Denison students interested in local food and I are visiting this creamery on a chilly Sunday afternoon just before milking time. Osage Lane Creamery is a goat dairy that makes handcrafted artisan cheeses.

Tom and Emma Stout of Osage Lane Creamery milk their herd of 25 goats twice a day during the season to support their artisanal cheese business.

Soon, afternoon milking will begin. With the season's kids now a few weeks old, the milking season is starting up again. Each year in late fall the ewes go dry, or stop producing milk, and with the help of the resident buck, they kid in the early months of February and March. Tom Stout, a soft-spoken burly man in his 50s, introduces us to Raspberry, Oil, Belt, and others. We are curious about these strange names, but Tom just laughs, for to him, each name fits each goat in some personal way. Goats, unlike most other farm animals, have extroverted personalities and insatiable curiosities, no doubt earning their deservedly strange names.

The milking herd, mainly mixed-breed brown goats of Nubian heritage with black tipped ears and legs, is Tom's signature blend, created over years of selective breeding. They are good milkers, he says. The nanny goats enjoy a fenced paddock in the barn where one door leads to the milking parlor and another to a grassy pasture outside. Both doors are closed now, but the parlor door is soon to open.

The spring babies, the kids, as baby goats are called, are in preschool, so to speak, bouncing around together in their own small group pens where they eat and grow and perfect goat tricks like scrambling over the fence or squeezing through a corner gap, or climbing on the hay rack for a better view towards an approaching bucket of grain, or perhaps eyeing the route to a quick escape. Separated shortly after birth from their mothers and fed by hand, they watch the nannies, their mothers, return to work. But more than one kid has discovered that with just the right speed and placement, she can scramble over the fence and scamper around free as a bird, looking for mom or just cruising around. One especially tiny kid, long black ears flopping, bounces along behind us with noisy pleas to pick her up. No one turns her down. In another few weeks, the kids will move on to new homes. Some will become goat meat, others farm pets or new additions to other milking herds. With an experienced eye, Tom will hand pick females with strong traits he likes to replenish his herd. In his full production season, about nine months long, he milks 25 goats every day, twice a day, morning and afternoon.

Tom and Emma Stout own and operate Osage Lane Creamery, a certified cheese production facility on the family farm Tom's father bought in 1946. They make raw milk cheeses: traditional Feta, a hard Hansen cheese from a recipe based on an Italian tome, and the newly popular flavored spreadable cheeses. Their cheese is made entirely from milk from their own goats. It is artisan cheese, made by Emma's experienced hand in distinctive flavors she creates including the spreadable blended flavors like horseradish, cranberry, orange, and tomato basil.

Food has historically been a major industry in Ohio. But as the farm and food economy restructured to favor cash grain crops when federal agricultural policy began to subsidize commodity crops, billions of food dollars left the state. Under current economic conditions, unfortunately, the lack of capital, contracts with corporate producers gone bad, expensive equipment, health and safety regulations that increase operating costs, transportation, and labor costs all conspire to dissuade small-scale farmers like the Stouts from persisting.

But as interest in local food rises, handcrafted goat cheese is one of those home-produced products that is claiming an

Emma makes wheels of raw-milk goat cheese, an unpasteurized cheese recognized for its nutritional and health benefits, in her cheese production facility.

increasing market. The Stouts have found a niche and they are pressing forward to find new ways to connect and collaborate. While there are more than 100 commercial goat cheese producers in the U.S. the real number is unknown because artisanal and farmstead cheese made by people like the Stouts are difficult to identify and count. In a national inventory of goats in the 2002 agricultural census, Ohio ranked tenth with more than 45,000 goats for meat and milk production.

These artisanal cheese makers sell their products at farmers markets, in small retail settings, and through direct sales, including CSAs and Internet sales. Like the Stouts, they tend to raise their own goats, maintain small herds, and use the milk for cheese or fluid goat milk. Raw milk cheese, made from unpasteurized milk, is regarded as a health food product and many seek its flavor and nutritional benefits. Emma values these raw milk cheeses for the healthy natural bacteria that enhance the flavors and that she believes develop a sound immune system. Although pasteurizing, or heating, is a method to control bacterial growth, raw-milk cheese is considered safe for sale and consumption after a cold storage period. The Stouts age their cheese in a walk-in cooler for the required 60 days before taking it to market.

෴

Since the day 20 years ago when a cancer-stricken young woman asked the Stouts if they could provide her with goat milk as she desperately sought ways to push back on her disease, the Stouts have had goats. "I couldn't tell a dying woman that I wouldn't help her," Tom said. To that end, he bought a milk goat, an old Toggenberg breed named Josie, and her non-milking companion, a horned Alpine goat named Nan. Tom, with Josie's help, provided Bethany with milk until the day the disease beat her a year later.

Josie had twins the next year, Marka and Kathy, and the family story with its twists and turns of fate and decisions that led finally to Osage Lane Creamery began. It's a story of trial and error, of success and failure, of adjusting, persevering, and sacrificing. Beneath it all, a deeply rooted passion for goats and the milk they produce kept them connected. As the interest in local foods soars, especially the interest in goat cheeses among a younger generation more tolerant, more willing to experiment, the Stouts finally see people looking to them for the good healthy food they have been producing for more than a decade. The path forward that includes the hopeful prospect, finally, of making and sustaining a profit, is brighter, but with the ups and downs of many years under their belt, they know it all remains uncertain.

Like those paths they have walked over the last twenty years, hope brightens and dims, sometimes on a daily basis. But experience, faith, and unbinding trust that the local food movement will continue to flourish in a time when the centralized food industry struggles with issues of long distance transportation, animal treatment, hormone additives, and a host of other now public issues, helps them press on. They want nothing more than to make good healthy food and a little profit on the side. The time may be right.

The present Osage Lane Creamery grew out of a failed fluid milk business. When the Stouts bought their own buck goat, Josie and her companions became seven. "We already had plenty of milk, then," Tom said. "We were throwing so much of it away every day. We tried lots of things to use the surplus, making ice cream and cheese on the top of the stove, but there was just too much."

An opportunity to buy a commercial herd with a connection to a reliable processor found the Stouts completely committed to turning their interest in fluid goat milk into a business. "Before we just grew vegetables and sold eggs," Tom said. "Now we were going to own a commercial dairy." In this turnkey operation, a herd of 100 goats and all the equipment was ready to go. The Stout family picked up and moved with the intention to buy the land and buildings along with the business. It didn't take long to realize they were in over their heads.

"It was just a man killer," Tom added. The farm was just cobbled together and "about as unhandy as it could be." It took everybody in our family, at least three of us, just to do the daily milking, he said. With the bucks and kids, they would have 130 head on hand at least. At kidding time, that number easily would grow to 200.

Less than 14 months later, they knew the deal had been a poor choice for their family. They backed out and moved back to the family farm where they live now. With their own small herd intact, they built the 40-foot by 130-foot hoop barn and dairy facility we walked into that afternoon.

With a smaller, more manageable herd, they joined a 25-farm member dairy cooperative called the Buckeye Valley Co Op. Large stainless steel milk trucks would lumber down their gravel drive, dodging melon-sized green wrinkled fruit called the Osage Orange, or more commonly referred to among farm folk as "hedge apples," to collect their milk on regular routes to member farms. Once collected, the milk was trucked to Wisconsin for processing. There, the French company, Bongrain USA, best known for its big brand dairy cheese name, Aloutte, homogenized, pasteurized, bottled, and loaded it onto trucks for wider distribution. Bongrain is mainly a cow dairy operation with goat's milk as just a small part of the business. The fluid goat's milk went mostly to the East Coast where it was more commonly known and appreciated for its healthful qualities and as a substitute for cow's milk for those who found themselves lactose intolerant. But in the Midwest, Tom believes that old wives' tales about goats eating tin cans, for example, and with milk as odiferous as the goats were lingered, further diminishing the development of a local market for goat milk and cheese.

"Those dairy days with the Co Op were pretty lucrative at first. The goats paid for themselves that first year." Contractual agreements over time presented challenges to Tom and his dairy though. "We had to trick the goats into breeding off season," he said. "It's just not natural for them to be year-round milkers. We had to sign a letter of intent that we would ship milk year round. But that didn't match with when the goats want to be dry. It's like the tree in winter that wants to be brown when we want it to be green."

When the milk truck arrived every three days to collect the Stouts' milk, their milk was pumped in with other milk. The truck goes on to the next farm, gathers that milk and so on until it is full. Then it headed for Wisconsin. But it only takes one load of high bacteria milk, milk that isn't properly cooled after milking, to contaminate the entire load. The bacteria in this "hot milk" increase exponentially, doubling every 20 minutes and by the time it reaches its destination, pasteurization at high temperatures is the only was to save it. "It's really a problem with transporting milk long distances over many days," Tom said. "And it's the reason why commercial milk is so highly pasteurized. When our milk got to the plant in Wisconsin," Tom said, "it was at least seven days old."

"But we thought this business would be good for a very long time," Tom said, unaware that the rug was about to be pulled from beneath them. Less than a year later, the Stouts received a letter from Bongrain USA ending their contract in 30 days. "Ohio milk had gotten too expensive to ship," the letter said. Tom rationalized the bad news. "Eventually, the price of diesel fuel would have killed us anyway." It was costing $2,000 to ship a load of milk to the plant in Wisconsin and when the company built a new plant even farther north, the gap widened. Growing dependence on cheap fossil fuels since the 1950s that created an infrastructure for long distance transportation of food was already beginning to fail at the producer level. Small farms felt the impact early. It would get worse before it got better.

Once the Wisconsin contract ended, everyone in the co-op was looking for a reason to quit, Tom said. "Farmers got rid of their goats. There was no place to sell the milk. We went from twenty-five farms to five in a month." For a time, the remaining farms were able to pick up another market in Minnesota but they were paying a milk broker $10,000 a year in retainer fees, and the participating farms, now dispersed over a larger geographic area, made the deal short-lived. Once again, transportation undercut profits.

The co-op disbanded.

But none of this affected the goats. They were still producing, Tom was still milking full bore and they were once again throwing milk on the ground, lots of it.

"For almost a year, we dumped a ton of milk on the ground week after week. We didn't have a choice. We were always hoping, always hoping that we'd get a phone call saying there was a market. We didn't want to fail." Like other local families growing and producing food on a small scale, the Stouts reached a point where they had to make a decision. Adjust and persevere, find a way forward or get out. Goats had become their life, their identity, Emma said. It was the common thread in their family. The lifestyle was hard to give up.

Other small local food producers, for similar reasons, faced the same choices in the 80s and 90s. They sensed they could only thrive if they learned to do business in a more cooperative manner. The farmers market venue provided that cluster opportunity and artisan cheese makers, like the Stouts, have found an audience for their product. As the interest in local food grows in Granville, the Stouts business grows, too. The Stouts also now sell their cheese through a local CSA, at the local grocery store, and at some retail locations in Columbus, further expanding their market access. Together, and with others in their cluster, they are able to respond to the hunger Americans have for buying good food from local farmers they know and trust.

∾

Emma had always experimented with cheese using the goat milk they had on hand every day. She had a knack. When the market for fluid milk dried up, Tom looked at what was left of the original 1850s house sitting just behind the 1917 home Tom grew up in and where Tom and Emma now raised their family. That homestead house would become Emma's cheese making facility, Tom decided.

Tom works a full-time job as an electrician. In addition to the 40-hour work-week and the daily milking chores, he carved out time to convert the old house into a 16 x 50-foot cheese plant. "I wanted to keep the building for its history," he said. But the renovations to the old structure proved so extensive that he ended up salvaging only the roof and one wall. It was enough though for Tom to feel he was keeping the family history alive. With the exception of pouring concrete, Tom did all of the work himself with friends and family.

Despite the challenge of building the plant, buying equipment, getting licenses, and learning how to make quality cheese for resale, the biggest obstacle continued to be finances. "Bankers understand car loans, home loans, but nothing about agriculture," Tom said. "Here's two people sitting across the table telling them they want to milk goats and make cheese and the banker is sitting there tapping his fingers thinking how can I get rid of these people."

The Stouts have over $40,000 invested in their local cheese business and Tom is proud to say this is a number held down by careful buying and re-using. It includes the work to convert the old house, the stainless steel kettle salvaged from a school, a cooler salvaged from a McDonald's restaurant, a tank water heater, stainless steel buckets, tables, and other equipment, all bought second-hand, and supplies needed to make from 60–80 pounds of cheese a week.

Emma became a student of cheese making. She visited other cheese facilities, took classes, and designed her workspace to be clean, efficient, and manageable. Every time she enters the plant, she puts on her white coat and hairnet, the garb of responsible food preparation. Outside shoes are banned. Everyone complies or they don't enter. She spends most of her days inside the production room, a warm, pleasantly fragrant place where she stirs fresh milk in a kettle the size of a stove, dips out measured amounts, and pours off the whey over and over until a Ricotta like consistency forms. In time, she will cut, wrap, and store chunks of the raw milk cheese in the cooler for ripening, and eventually package them for sale.

Cheese is in demand year round, with stronger sales in winter than summer, Tom said. Even though the goats are dry several months of the year, Emma makes enough cheese during the milking season to meet demand year round. She is working to improve packaging and labeling to make her product more appealing on the store shelf and on their farmers market table.

She admits her biggest challenge is marketing. While Emma and Tom handle a barn full of goats and operate a highly controlled production facility in compliance with the Ohio Department of Health (ODH) and the USDA, the Stouts are still learning the strategies of sales and promotion. They do know that the shrink-wrap packaging style and simple stick-on label they currently use is suitable for preservation and identification, but adds little to presentation. They're working on that.

"All of this is a struggle for everyone, this small food thing," said Tom. "People have this romantic notion about local food, but the amount of work, the lack of funds, the labor — all the issues. No one realizes the real cost of local food."

Tom lies in bed at night, he says, wide awake, wondering if they are doing the right thing. The sacrifices: nice things for their home, new cars, are hard to take sometimes. But there's no victory in quitting, he says. "I get up at the crack of dawn just as the sun is rising to go out to the goats and I know it's worth it."

Sidebar 2

Ohio's Early Agricultural History

Ohio includes the first lands of the Northwest Territory to be settled following the Revolutionary War and reveals a uniquely complex settlement history. Ohio's early settlement spanned a series of congressional acts culminating in the Land Act of 1796 that formalized the Rectangular Land Survey system, which was then applied to all federal lands west of Ohio. It helps explain the dense rectangular road network throughout the Midwest that facilitates movement of agricultural materials and allows for relatively foolproof rural navigation. Briefly, the system is based on six-by-six-mile named townships subdivided into 36 one-square-mile sections numbered along rows beginning in the northeast corner and ending in the southeast. The townships are spatially organized in east-west bands of Townships extending north and south of Base Lines and north-south Ranges extending east and west of Principal Meridians so, for example, a 40-acre parcel in Van Wert County in NW Ohio may have the designation NW ¼, SW ¼, Section 35, T2S, R3E of the 1st Principal Meridian and Base Line.

Ohio itself is a surveying hodge-podge with some areas following various iterations of the Rectangular Land Survey and others, for example the Virginia Military District in the southwestern part of the state, following the

British metes and bounds system based on local topo-graphic markers. Symmes (between the Miami rivers) Purchase was surveyed by magnetic north rather than geographic north with townships extending east-west and ranges north-south. The Granville area and Licking County are part of the U.S. Military District that utilizes uncommon five-by-five-mile townships with an inconsistent survey of smaller subdivisions.

For agricultural settlement, the cost and minimum acreage of land available for purchase was far more important than the actual arrangement of townships and sections. The Harrison Land Act of 1800 reduced minimum acreage for purchase to 320 acres (a half section) from 640 acres and provided for credit opportunities in order to promote land acquisition by individuals rather than land companies and speculators. But 320 acres of wooded land was much too large for a family to farm and at $2/acre the initial investment was very high. The minimum acreage was subsequently reduced to 160 acres in 1804, to 80 acres in 1820 and to 40 acres in 1832, which with a minimum price of $1.25/acre resulted in a much more manageable $50 threshold price. Virtually all land in Ohio, and Indiana and Illinois as well, was purchased before the Homestead Act of 1863. By 1876, the last public land office in Ohio had closed, marking the end of frontier settlement in the state. According to the 1880 U.S. Census, 94% of Ohio's lands were then in farms, exceeding that of any other state and attesting to the good quality of Ohio's soils and the efficient transport network that had evolved.

Ohio developed some regional agricultural specializations based on water transportation links, topographic controls, and soil quality. For example, the lands of the Connecticut Reserve in the northeast focused on dairy, the productive wet prairies of the Scioto Plain south of Columbus had the largest farms, which concentrated on corn-fed beef cattle, while in the southwest corn-hog farming dominated the Miami valleys earning Cincinnati the title of Porkopolis. Here the standard Midwestern three-year crop rotation of corn, wheat or other small grain, and hay was developed and held sway until the advent of commercial fertilizers after WW II. The less productive soils of the hilly, unglaciated southeast were largely in pasture supporting beef cattle with wheat production on valley floors of the Muskingum drainage system. The flat, poorly drained lands of the Maumee watershed and western Lake Erie shoreline resisted settlement until drainage tiling was emplaced in the decades following the Civil War. These lands were to become some of the most productive in the state with a significant amount of vegetable production in addition to cash-grain farming.

Topographically, centrally located Licking County is a microcosm of the state, possessing most broad soil types and terrain elements from gently undulating till plains in the west to localized lacustrine plains in the south to hilly end moraines to flat outwash terraces in the central valleys to unglaciated bedrock-controlled hill country in the east. The 1840 census indicates that Licking County already had a well-diversified agricultural economy ranking 5th in wheat, 9th in corn, 4th in beef cattle, and 7th in dairy among Ohio counties. With significant development pressure from an expanding Columbus metropolitan area aside, the county retains its agricultural importance, ranking 6th in agricultural sales in 2007, which given Ohio's agricultural balance only accounts for about 2% of the state's production.

— Tod Frolking

Chapter 3

Back to the Future

*Farming has the potential to go through the greatest upheaval
since the Green Revolution . . . driven not by a nostalgic bid to
revert to the agrarian ways of our ancestors, but by looking
towards the future, leapfrogging past the age of heavy machinery
and pollution to take advantage of the sun's free energy and use
the waste of one species as food for another.*

— Chef Dan Barber
"Change We Can Stomach," *New York Times,* 2008

In Defense of Food by Michael Pollan was on the New
York Times bestseller list for 27 weeks in 2008. Pollan's earlier
national bestseller *The Omnivore's Dilemma,* stood at the top
of the bestseller list for more than two years. He has authored
seven other books on food and gardening and is easily the
most recognized face and voice in the movement, coining such
expressions as "You are what what you eat eats," "Don't eat
anything your great-grandmother wouldn't recognize as food,"
and "edible food-like substance."

◀ Kathy and Rich Harrison stand with Frosty Flake, a Belted Galloway X
cow, in one of their carefully managed pastures at Skipping Stone Farm.

53

Two million copies of award-winning novelist Barbara Kingsolver's 2007 *Animal, Vegetable, Miracle: A Year of Food Life*, have been sold. In the story, Kingsolver recounts her family's year off from their regular lifestyle to grow their own food and eat locally. The nonfiction book has won numerous prizes including the James Beard award. *Food, Inc.,* a documentary on the food industry by noted film director Robert Kenner, and several others, like *King Corn* and *Fresh*, for example, have captured the attention of millions who viewed them at mainstream theatres and at college or community showings. They now stream on the Internet.

Farmer "celebrity" Joel Salatin finds his Polyface Farm in Virginia a bit of a tourist attraction these days with his story of sustainable farming first brought to light in Pollan's *Omnivore's Dilemma*. He later appeared in *Food, Inc.* and has gained a reputation as the author of his own books and as a voice on the lecture circuit. Salatin at one time refused to sell his meat to anyone who lived more than 100 miles from his farm.

Statewide conferences, such as the two-day Ohio Ecological Food and Farm Association (OEFFA) conference held in Granville sells out every year to many hundreds of farmers and those interested in natural and local food systems. Prominent names in the food movement like Woody Tasch, chairman of Slow Money, a national network organized around new ways to think about food, money, and soil are keynote speakers. Pollan and Salatin have been past speakers.

I teach a course at Denison University to first year students where we learn the ropes of academic essay writing by looking at the food industry and its alternatives. Other courses

at the liberal arts college also address food through economics, culture, environment, and literature. Nearby Kenyon
College's *Food for Thought* initiative directed by the Rural Life
Center strives to connect students with local food producers.
The Granville Exempted Village Schools is heralded for its
Farm to School lunch program started four years ago where
33% of all the district's food for 2,500 students now comes
from farms within 50 miles and where nearly 70% of all students eat the school lunch, up from 25% before the program
began. A school garden supplements the fresh vegetables coming from local CSAs. "Food speak" is everywhere in this central Ohio town and across the state, and for the small-scale
farmer on the ground, organic or not, ready or not, it is usher-
ing in a new life.

Kathy and Rich Harrison own a 96-acre farm just miles
outside of Granville. "Suddenly, everyone is calling us asking
for grass-fed beef like it's some new thing," Kathy says, "and
grass grazing has been around here for fifteen years." Or, she
gets calls or emails from new customers to order a side of beef
and she replies, "Can you wait until 2014?"

The energy, the momentum, the hype around food the
way Kathy has been eating it since she was five years old is
astounding to the Harrisons who raise Belted Galloway X and
mixed-breed cattle, chickens, and, most recently, turkeys. Now,
Kathy says, they call this food "organic," and "grass grazed"
and "free range." The Harrisons, like most farmers, see themselves as ordinary people who just have a passion for the land,
the quality and cleanness of the food it produces, and the lifestyle
it offers. They want good food for themselves and are eager to

share with others. As business booms, they are enjoying a new limelight they may have never expected.

Kathy is an organic chemist. "In my early 20s in college and thereafter I was very much hooked into the whole chemical thing – using Round Up and fertilizers. But I got away from that when I started reading and remembering my dad as a farmer. All of the synthetic inputs are wrecking the soil structure and the critters that are beneficial to creating the nutrients. My dad, who was my role model and started raising our meat when I was five years old, never used noxious chemicals so now I wasn't going to either. It was like going back to the future," she said.

While Kathy lived the country life as a child and grew up farming, her husband, Rich, has come to it from a distance. With degrees in math and chemistry and an MBA, he lived and worked in urban settings until he met Kathy. An imposing 1893 red brick Victorian house that "seems like we've been renovating forever," Kathy says, anchors the Harrison's Skipping Stone Farm. The house and its farm buildings sit nearly two-thirds of a mile off a township road in north central Licking County. Like farming, Kathy values past knowledge and experience as passionately as she embraces new developments that make farming easier and more successful. She runs her farm respectful of what each has to offer.

William and Orlean Smoots built the house for entertaining purposes during the time William was running for state office. He lost the election, his 16-year-old son was killed when he tried to hop a train to get a ride into a neighboring town and after that, the family seemed to disintegrate. The

56

family, with remaining daughter, Alta, lived there for only a short time with caretakers on the property for many years after. One of those, Leonard Neighbarger, tenant and share-cropper in 1972 when Alta died, bought the house and 100 acres at auction. Leonard raised hogs and the grain to feed them. Kathy bought the property from him in 1994. "He had a real penchant for using old worn out garden hose buried underground for his hog water lines — I don't know how many Leonard Artesian Wells we fixed before decommissioning the original water main in 2011 and putting in a new one," Kathy laughed. The old wooden barn, which had burned down in the 1970s or 80s, was replaced with a metal-sided barn that now occupies the footprint, sitting atop the original floor. Originally a bank barn, it retained that function and is open sided on the lower ground level for cows to wander in and out.

Next door a shed building is home to a flock of chickens who roam the yard producing dozens of eggs a week, most of which Kathy sells to the local green grocer store in Granville. "I'm to the point that I can't keep up with demand," she says, "I'm doing eight dozen a week and they want more." From other chickens they raise, they also have meat in their freezer. They are scaling up to provide whole chickens to the store for customers who have been asking for them.

Kathy and Rich attend the OEFFA conference every year and they stay current with the literature being written on the food movement. They have both read Kingsolver's *Animal, Vegetable, Miracle* among the works of other new and renewed voices in this food movement. In the author's voice, the book chronicles the Kingsolver's move from the desert city of Tucson to her husband's old family farm in Virginia where they and their two daughters commit to growing their own food for one year. There are many "miracles" in this story as the title implies, but one that the Harrisons remember clearly is the story of the family's turkey experiences. "Of the 400 million turkeys Americans consume each year, more than 99% of them are a single breed: the Broad Breasted White, a quick fattening monster bred specifically for the industrial-scale setting," Kingsolver writes. These birds, the main event at the Thanksgiving table and now a regular staple in the meat departments of grocery stores year round, have been selected, modified, and are factory farmed solely on the size of their breasts for the white meat Americans have come to prefer. The genetically modified birds kept in confined feeding operations can't mate and by the time they are a few months old are too front-heavy to stand or walk.

The diversity of the turkey species was in trouble. Old breeds, the ancestors of the modern Broad Breasted White, were disappearing under a relentless industrial market. By the 1960s the heritage breed turkey had been driven from the market. By 1990, the original breeds were nearly gone.

Kingsolver was interested in preserving and protecting a breed and in producing meat of exceptional quality for her family. Slowly in this new world of food and farming, farmers typified by Kingsolver try their hand at raising breeds — now called heritage breeds — beyond the end of November where the commercial bird meets its end after only about 18 weeks of life. To raise turkeys and create breeding programs requires knowledge, patience, and a lot of luck. Turkeys are more disease prone than chickens and the longer they are kept, the more that can befall them. As Kingsolver says, they are a "dickens to raise." She turned to old texts on animal husbandry for advice many times and especially when one of her hens began to act strangely, becoming droopy and walking around dragging her wings. She discovered through her reading that her hen wasn't sick as she thought she must surely be, but rather in the mood to become a mother. In time, 10 eggs hatched and Kingsolver and her daughter, Lily, were struck by the miracle of the moment. "Crazed and giddy, there in the dusty barn, we held hands and danced. Babies! That was all, and that was enough. A nest full of little ding-dongs, and time begins once more."

According to the Heritage Turkey Foundation, there are 10 breeds of turkeys that are endangered but beginning to make a comeback. Farmers, like the Kingsolvers and locally the Harrisons and others, are beginning to raise them, gradually reacquainting the public with the taste and texture of "real" turkey meat. Of those ten recognized breeds, Kingsolver choose the Bourbon Red. Heritage breeds are bred for flavor, beauty, self-reliance, and hardiness. The Bourbon Red is a large, reddish-brown bird with white accents on its feathers. They are scrappy, resourceful, sturdy, and independent. The male display is striking as the bird spreads it white tail and wing feathers. It's the kind of turkey children envision and draw and color for those homemade tablemats at Thanksgiving.

When Kathy and Rich read Kingsolver's story of raising the Bourbon Red, they decided to give it a try. Well, sort of, Kathy will chuckle. "The reason we have turkeys is because I wanted hogs," she laughs. "Just two or three to start, to churn up the cow manure in the barn and create good compost." But

This Bourbon Red tom turkey, a heritage breed now popularized by many small-scale farmers, rules the roost in the turkey yard.

Rich, not being a hog fan, slipped smoothly into diversionary mode and managed to peak Kathy's interest in heritage breed turkeys as a business venture, recognizing the growing interest in the free range and heritage breed turkeys. They bought their first batch of turkey hatchlings, or poults, three years ago to test the waters of raising the birds for customers.

"Turkeys aren't like chickens," Kathy realized when the tiny birds started dropping dead. "Chicks come wired to peck so they peck and eat and drink naturally. We finally realized that poults don't. Although they don't scratch like chicks, they looked like they were eating and drinking, but they weren't."

When faced with a problem, and problems with animals can strike hard and fast leading to quick death, Kathy looks for advice. She found that modern husbandry practice calls for keeping young turkey poults separate from baby chicks to prevent transmission of disease, but that wasn't working. She started reading, reaching for old texts on animal husbandry, texts that might include discussions of raising these now rare breeds. What she found countered current thought. From a 1907 bulletin from the Western Washington Experiment Station: "Unlike chicks the young poults appeared not to know where to find their food. Teaching them to eat promised to become quite a challenge. Failing to attract them to their feed in other ways, a few young chicks were placed in the nursery with each flock of poults. It was surprising how aptly they took their first lessons from the chicks." Kathy beamed, "Within one hour the problem was solved and all were feeding and drinking with no further trouble." In another old text, she read, "It takes five chicks to raise a turkey." She's a believer in that now.

"So I didn't care what the modern stuff said because I wasn't raising the commercial turkey. I divided the chicks and the turkeys into small groups and put them together. Wonder of wonders, the turkeys started to thrive. They will imprint on the chicks, the readings suggested, and like the chicks, will

61

actually eat and drink. And they did. It's like an old generation coming out of hiding," she said.

That first batch of poults, its number now reinforced with
new recruits, produced a dozen healthy birds. Of those birds,
three broody hens and a Tom were kept to start a breeding
flock. Another became their Thanksgiving dinner and they
processed and sold the rest, their nudge into the turkey market. "They're good mothers," Kathy said of her new breeding
flock. "The poults just follow their mother and eat and drink
just as she does. It's so easy now." As subsequent generations
of the Bourbon Reds are hatched and raised, the Harrisons
see a niche market developing for their Skipping Stone Farm.

The Harrison's Skipping Stone Farm is a member of
OEFFA. In the organization's directory, the farm is listed this
way: "Skipping Stone Farm occupies 96 acres of fertile bot-
tom land along the North Fork of the Licking River. Our
Belted Galloway X cattle are raised on sod-building perennial
polyculture pastures, clean well water, natural minerals, fresh
air and sunshine."

In this new world of grass grazing popularity, clean farming, and real food, the Harrison's typify the small-scale Ohio
farmer who raises livestock for a local food market, and who is
respectful of the land and the environment. They use the language of a new generation of farmers in describing their beef,
calling it Salad Bar Beef, meaning not that it's beef you'll
find at a salad bar, but rather lean beef from cows that have
enjoyed a diet of "salad bar" pasture: grasses, legumes, and
forbs (herbaceous flowering plants), diets free of hormones or
antibiotics, or other "synthetic gunk" as Kathy calls it. At farmers

markets or through personal searches, locavores look for meat from animals humanely raised on healthy grass pastures. They may not know necessarily why grass fed animals make better tasting, more nutritious meat, but they do now know that animals force fed conventionally grown GMO grains with added antibiotics and hormones is something they want to avoid. By looking to traditional farming practices and capitalizing on modern knowledge of animal husbandry, the Harrisons and others like them use the best of both worlds to develop sound farming practices in this time of food awareness. In this process, they enjoy getting to know their customers and that face-to-face relationship builds trust.

County health departments in Ohio regulate the sale of fresh meat, dairy, and eggs at farmers markets. Rules vary, but for meat, the trend is requiring farmers to scale up in refrigeration equipment in order to sell there. One farmer hooks a car battery to a small chest freezer in the back of his pickup truck to meet the basic requirement. Others must invest in expensive refrigerated trucks. The Harrisons, as others, have chosen not to sell at farmers markets to avoid these expensive and cumbersome restrictions. Instead, they market their beef, eggs, and poultry through several wholesale and retail outlets and, most commonly, directly from their farm through word of mouth. Interestingly, as the Harrisons get to know their customers, they discover they've often come to them having read Kingsolver's book or others in this new niche of food writing. "They know what they want and now they feel safe about what they're eating," Kathy says. "They want to know where their food comes from. They want a face on their food."

The Harrisons are most proud of their Belted Galloway X cattle, an old Scottish breed that Kathy fell in love with as a college student. Their unique appearance, a red, dun, or black body with a wide white "belt" around the middle catches your eye when you drive onto the farm and see the pasture ahead. Most of the Harrison's "Belties," or "my Oreo cows," as Kathy lovingly calls them, feature this genetic trait, a black body with a wide, white belt, the original color pattern of the cattle. Over the years, breeding diversification produced red and dun colors as well so the Harrison herd is mixed. Their herd also has some crossbred cattle from their two bulls to keep the lineage genetically diverse. The Belted Galloway's first recorded history appears to have been in the 16th Century in the former Galloway district of southwestern Scotland. These sturdy cows with thick coats of hair may have arrived when Dutch travelers brought the Dutch Belted cow north and across the English Channel from the Low Countries.

The Belties are ideal for a grass-grazing environment, Kathy says. A double coat of hair provides winter protection, allowing them to survive harsh environments. The Harrison's rotate their pastures regularly and plans are to begin to move their chickens in behind the cows to scratch up the manure left and compost the soil, a strategy they picked up from Salatin. "The cows wintered over just fine last year," Rich said, noting that Ohio's fluctuating seasons, some exceptionally warm, others very cold and some persistently wet present a challenge. Just recently, Ohio's climate zone has been raised to a zone 6 meaning warmer low temperatures can be expected. "Last year, we had more problems with mud than freezing because the ground never really deeply froze," he said. They feed some hay in the winter but grain isn't necessary.

Beltie meat is lean and flavorful, Kathy says. "If our customers want lean meat, we take the cows in at 18 months. For more marbled meat, they go at 30 months." But as important as the quality of the meat and the beauty and practicality of the cows for the Harrisons is their disposition. Belties are calm natured. "We don't want anyone to get hurt," Rich says. "Cows are big 2,000 pound animals and they can damage things." Through careful breeding and culling and meeting the needs of their customers, the Harrisons have built a herd of healthy, gentle animals. "I want to be able to turn my back on a bull and feel safe," Rich said.

Old time farmers often recommend not naming livestock animals. They are not pets and are destined for the freezer at some point in their life, usually early on, so better not to get too familiar. Kathy and Rich, however, dismiss this and have names for everything on the farm: Bling Bling, Hedda Hopper, Gerkin, Swiss Miss, Zucchini, Sweet Baby Ray, Loafie, McRib, Frosty, Cappuccino, Latte, Rock Candy. They love names and can rattle off a list dizzyingly rapid fire. And the cows are on teams: the A Team, the B Team, and the F Team, (F for freezer). The Harrisons love their animals in a realistic way. Yes, they will be on someone's dinner table one day, but when they're at Skipping Stone Farm, they are part of the community of dogs, chickens, turkeys, and cows. If the livestock animals behave themselves, they may enjoy a long life. "When you take on animals, you have an obligation to take care of them," Rich said. Each one is important and contributes to the Harrison's farm life in some way. Their farm's website has a tribute page to long-loved and now gone cows from their herd.

In their farming life, Kathy and Rich continually look for ways to be more efficient. "Find ways to let the animals do the work," Rich says. It takes nearly two hours to bed down the barn with fresh straw, for example. One day when they were pressed for time they dragged a 500-pound round bale of red clover hay and straw mix into the barn for the cows to eat. The next day to their amazement, Rich says, "the cows played soccer with that bale of hay," pushing it around, eating what they wanted and spreading the rest. Job completed.

"We like to eat healthy," Rich says. Both Harrisons teach part time at the local college in Newark, the county seat, and supplement their income with their farm business. Rich adds, "For us, it's a good time to expand. The grass fed beef scene is growing like crazy."

Sidebar 3

Wrought by ice

Ohio's agricultural fertility, and that of the agricultural lands through the Midwest, is due to a geologically brief 10,000-year visit by a massive ice sheet that finally met its demise in northern Canada a scant 7,000 years ago. Surprisingly, a key player in the ice sheet's success was the Gulf of Mexico which fed the glacier with moisture (snowfall) and allowed it to grow and flow southward almost to Cincinnati, the farthest south a continental glacier reached anywhere on earth. Across the Midwest, the ice extended south in great lobes following broad lowlands developed on weak sedimentary rocks, the major basins that now hold the Great Lakes. The south flowing ice scoured and plucked the hard rocks of Canada's continental shield then added the more easily eroded sedimentary bedrock and soft sediments from the Great Lakes region and deposited much of this sediment near its southern margin, that is in Ohio. In humid environments like Ohio, soils weather and lose vital nutrients over time so in some respects youth equals vitality. From a soil perspective, the 14,000 years since the glacier departed from Ohio is fairly young.

Ohio reveals the strong impacts that modest differences in terrain had on the ice advance. In the northeast, the southward flowing Ontario-Erie lobe was forced to climb the Allegheny escarpment and could barely crest the Great Lakes divide to an east-west line from southern Richland to central Columbiana County, leaving east and southeast Ohio unglaciated. In contrast, in the west the Huron-Erie lobe flowed far southward on weaker and lower-lying limestones and shales, and was split into the Miami and Scioto sub-lobes by the topographic high in Logan County. Glaciers were quite sloppy in their work, leaving complex depositional sequences of unsorted dense glacial till, fine-grained lake deposits, and porous sand and gravel outwash. Overall, glaciers produced a much flatter Ohio with thick deposits filling formerly deep bedrock valleys.

Licking County, in east-central Ohio, actually saw ice advance from the west as the Scioto sub-lobe expanded eastward onto the rugged Appalachian Plateau like batter spreading on a waffle iron. Fortunately, the glacial tills in Licking County contain pulverized shale and limestone, scraped up and carried by the ice eastward from bedrock to the west in the Scioto basin, that provide natural fertility. The till also contains the coarser local siltstone and sandstone bedrock and a fair number of long-distance travelers, the Canadian erratic cobbles and boulders that now decorate lawns and fields. These till deposits form flat to gently undulating ground moraine in the western third of the county, lands that generally require field tiling to improve drainage. Further east, as the local relief increases, the glacier left a complex mosaic of till-mantled uplands and ridges; steep slopes with shallow rocky soils, broad well-drained sand and gravel outwash terraces; and flat, often poorly-drained, lacustrine plains that are very productive when drained. Thus the county showcases most of the types of glacial terrains and deposits that are found statewide and modern agricultural land use clearly reflects this diversity.

— Tod Frolking

Chapter 4

The Tipping Point

Every aspect of our lives is, in a sense, a vote for the kind of world we want to live in.

— Frances Moore Lappé
Sharing the Harvest: A Citizen's Guide to Community Supported Agriculture, 1999

At age 2, Lee Bird wanted to play with nothing but toy tractors, mostly green John Deere tractors. At age 9, with help from his parents, Lee bought his own real tractor, a 1939 John Deere. Never mind that he lived in a neighborhood in the middle of the city on a street with houses rather than fields. Never mind that other kids were riding bikes and throwing balls around as Lee climbed aboard his worthy stead.

"He would park that tractor in the driveway and he'd run it up and down, and then up and down in the alley behind the house," says his mother, Ann Bird. "Tractors were all he ever dreamt of."

Lee is 30 now. In jeans and rubber boots, we walk from high tunnel to high tunnel, six in all. It is a cloudy afternoon

The Bird family of Bird's Haven Farms stands in one of their six high tunnels that capture the sun and create the warmth to allow them to extend their growing season.

well beyond the end of the growing season, cool and muddy from days of rain. Most of the hooped structures, lined up like long caterpillars, stand barren now, tomatoes, lettuce, and cucumbers grown and harvested, earth as dry inside under plastic skies as it is soggy outside. A bright green skinny row of Swiss Chard with wide thick leaves on ruby stalks brightens a part of the tunnel we walk into. Because chard is a fall crop that can flourish in cooler temperatures, it will continue to produce for weeks to come. It may, in fact, survive the winter altogether.

These 90' long and 35' wide half round structures are poly covered translucent plastic stretched over steel frames. They capture sun and warmth, mini farm fields under cover for planting and growing. In the far one, straggly tomato plants linger, tired wilting vines still strung up by pulleys and cords, hung by their necks until dead, it seems. A few small fruits, some hoping to redden, dot the broad covered field, but for the most part, the tomato season, stretching amazingly from May through October inside the tunnel, has finally run its course. Two workers at the far end are cleaning up, freeing the vines from their nooses and carting them off. These 750 plants have been in the ground since April, a long season in Ohio by any tomato's standard. Tresseling the vines rather than staking minimizes disease and damage, and Lee has discovered that one planting will keep producing all season, a substantial savings in time, money, and labor.

Lee Bird and his sister, Bryn, are, like Erin, representative of a new generation of young farmers across the country, finding their place in a life on the land and defining a lifestyle. Unlike Erin in the first story, however, Lee and Bryn's family own their own land, a 100-acre family farm, a major asset to young farmers. Lee is the hands-on grower; Bryn the local food advocate working to expand access and develop broader markets for increasing production in an environment hungry for local food. If Bryn has her way, for example, regional food hubs will form across the state to give local farmers, like her brother, access to central distribution centers. Once farmers are able to meet the demand from farmers markets, they look to ramping up production, finding distribution markets, and hopefully, making a living wage.

It hasn't been easy to increase production and develop new markets; sometimes it feels like it won't get any easier. The largest challenge in the central Ohio area may be accessing the market, but there are others: securing operating capital and reliable steady labor, adding and upgrading growing houses and the technologies of specialty crop farming, facing the organic challenge, meeting soaring demand in a popular new market for local foods, and dealing with wildlife crop destruction, weeds, plant pests and diseases, and of course, the weather, all making the struggle that much harder. The family is about to put up their seventh high tunnel where they plan to grow raspberries. And to fill out the berry market, blueberry bushes are slated to join their popular strawberry field. In all, they have more than 40 acres in cultivation. With nips and tucks and a little bit of luck, Lee believes they are about to break through, to become a sustainable small-scale farm business.

∽

Pueblo, Colorado, the Birds' home for 20 years, was changing rapidly in the 1980s. Developments stuffed with houses shaped new suburbs and rural land evaporated along with the water. While Lee's father, Tom, enjoyed a successful veterinary business, he yearned to be closer to the ground. Tom had grown up on a farm in central Ohio. He loved the rich soil for what it could produce; he loved the water that Pueblo didn't have. In his life now, he wanted to be a farmer like his father had been.

When the Bird's two older children graduated from high school, it was time to go home, Tom decided. Lee was 12 then, Bryn was 10. The two older children were off to college. In 1995, Tom sold the practice and moved his family to a farm just outside of Granville. The dusty gravel road and distant neighbors marked a stark contrast to the modern suburban life the family had known, Ann remembers. The family lost no time in planting a backyard garden and getting a flock of chickens and a small herd of sheep. Ann, who grew up in Colorado, smiles when she talks about the garden she planted in those first years of adjusting to country life. "I was just astounded at the quantity of water there was here for a garden," she remarked.

From that small garden plot and the chickens that laid pastel colored bluish-green eggs, Ann gradually stepped out. Lee removed the bed of the family's old 1984 Toyota pickup and replaced it with a wooden platform and bins suitable for transporting and displaying produce, not unlike trucks that in earlier times would drive street to street hawking fresh produce. A bright green and white striped canopy made a tented roof so that when the sides open, the truck becomes its own sales stand. Bryn liked to call it the circus truck, her father laughed, but the truck, all dolled up and soon quickly recognizable, became the logo for the farm. It still sometimes takes Bird's Haven Farms to market.

Ann joined a handful of other gardeners about twenty years ago in setting up her card table at the newly formed Saturday market in Granville, held then in a parking lot behind the Methodist Church, a space once a park before it was paved over. It was called Petunia Park in Granville's earlier history. Maybe a dozen hobby gardeners would bring vegetables, flowers, jams, or, often in those days, their one crop. These one-crop weekend farmers became the green bean man or the corn man or known by whatever seasonal crop they grew. After the crop was finished, they were finished, too, gone with the season.

Even in those early days though, Ann planned her backyard garden to yield through the growing season so she could claim her spot at every Saturday market, which operated then for a few brief summer months. The seasons kept her table full: lettuce and spinach in June, beets and peppers in July, tomatoes in August, squash in September, pumpkins in October. One reliable item on her table, week after week, however, was the colored eggs laid by her Ameraucana chickens, sometimes called Easter Eggers because of the tinted bluish-green eggs they lay. For townies, most who had eaten white eggs all their lives, these colored eggs were quite a novelty and the tip of a local food awareness that was forming. At 8 A.M., customers trickled in, mostly older ladies and gents, toting their own bags for picking and choosing. The crowd was never large, but lively enough to give little Petunia Park the nice warm feeling of friends and neighbors out and about together on a Saturday morning gathering food for a meal or two.

Farmers markets have grown up since then as farmers respond to the growing demand for local food. As people turn aside from conventionally produced and grown food, on any Saturday anywhere in towns and cities across the country, markets are packed. Families make an outing of them. They bring their bags, their kids, and their dogs. Markets are food parties all summer long, candy stores of vegetables, breads, jams, flowers, and salsas. If you want homegrown peaches at the Granville Farmers Market, prepare to stand in line for a long time. If it's sweet corn you're after, there's another line waiting. And for heirloom tomatoes, get there really early. Friends are there too and the local coffee shop is happy to brew you a fresh cup of fair trade coffee as you stroll along. Bakers near by set out fresh muffins and breads. On the way home with loaded bags of produce, meat, cheese, and other foods, thoughts turn to enjoying this bounty for days to come.

For farmers, however, weekly markets have become competitive, sometimes hotly so, as bakers, produce growers, cheese makers, meat producers, and those who produce an array of value added products, like green veggie drinks, spices and salsas, set up displays to attract the attention of passers-by. The Granville Farmers Market, well known in Central Ohio, on any summer Saturday is so crowded it's difficult to negotiate a path from one end to the other. A Market Master, an employee of the local Chamber of Commerce, the sponsoring organization, organizes and monitors the weekly sale and oversees its operations. A committee of participating farmers work with the Market Master to set guidelines for operations. Bringing in produce not grown on their own farms, for example, is not permitted in this market and the Market Master trains a keen eye on his vendors each and every week, even visiting farms to observe their operation first hand. And Granville is just one of thousands of market towns. Across the country today, these popular sources of local fresh food sprawl across parking lots and community parks on Saturdays and mid-week days. They are the gathering place, the place where friends and neighbors meet to listen to music, maybe even dance a bit, and take home food for dinner. Local food is no longer just a card table in a small parking lot. Eating locally is now more widely recognized as a path to better health, a sustainable economy, a healthier environment, and a good community. Bird's Haven Farm, with Ann's long tenure at the market, occupies a prime double-sized space at the corner entrance, the old truck reliably opening its sides and expanding on long tables in both directions with produce spilling out and customers lining up. Like many other small-scale farmers who are ramping up production, the Birds do other markets during the week: Tuesday at Granville again, Wednesdays at Westerville in neighboring Franklin County, home to the state's capital city of Columbus. Many farmers do multiple markets, picking, packing, and setting up nearly every day of the week somewhere in central Ohio.

So young Lee and his sister, Bryn, spent their childhood working alongside their parents to define their passion for farming. In their backyard garden where Ann began growing food, young Lee planted a plot of corn. When he surprised himself by making more money selling bundles of spent corn stalks as fall decorations at the market than by taking the corn to the local feed mill, his interest in growing for people instead of animals peaked. Tom, himself, hadn't had much luck turning the land into commodity crops such as corn and soybeans. He gave it seven years. "We just didn't have enough land to compete," he said. With generally low commodity prices, conventional farmers in Ohio must plant many hundreds of acres of corn and soybeans to stay afloat. It is no longer possible for the small farmer with the typical small farm of a hundred acres or so to make a living on the land growing commodity crops. Feeling like pawns in the great agricultural machine, they turned to food. Lee was ready.

Lee graduated from college in 2005 with a degree in agricultural systems and management, a back-up career path, he admits, in case his dream of being a specialty crop farmer, as the USDA calls growing vegetables, failed. To celebrate his new venture, the Birds put up the first greenhouse. "This was the first year we really worked on a larger scale," he says.

Lee has a passion for the work and a handiness for cobbling things together. Each greenhouse and high tunnel came used from auction or from an owner leaving the business. Lee would dismantle the structures, haul them to the farm in pieces, and reassemble them. The first greenhouse came from an Amish farm seven years ago when that family relocated to Kentucky. Along with it came an Amish built wood-burning furnace to heat water that ran through old radiator fins and warmed the air inside the greenhouse. "When we first started, we were neophytes," Tom said of this new plastic culture, "and we were lucky. If we would have had to heat with propane as most greenhouses are heated, we couldn't have afforded it. So we've never used the expensive fuel. We still fuel our greenhouse furnace with slab wood and trees that come down on our property," he said.

When the greenhouses heat up, seedlings sprout in flats on tables and from hanging flower baskets on rails. "We move the seedlings to the high tunnels in March or so," Lee said. Last season, the family grew 500 hanging flower baskets in the greenhouse. Sales of flowering baskets are good, they plan to do more next season. Trial and error under the family's watchful conservative hands helps them nip and tuck the business.

Roadside, a small, open-sided market shed operates seasonally to welcome people that stop by for produce on off-market days or to pick their own strawberries or other produce in the fields. Someone working in the high tunnels, the greenhouses, or the fields will magically appear when customers arrive. Inside, tables are filled with what is growing: round yellow Yukon potatoes or long narrow fingerlings; red and yellow beets; peppers of all sizes, shapes and colors; and, of course, heirloom tomatoes, the farm's biggest crop. In the fall, mountains of pumpkins and winter squash mark the stand as cars top the rise in the road. Baskets and cutters are available for those who find their way down that dusty gravel road and want to pick their own vegetables or flowers. The Pick Your Own trend and even the roadside stand, popular venues over the last 20 years or so, has eased though, Ann says, as farmers

Lee and Bryn Bird, the brother-sister team that is making Bird's Haven Farm a viable business, work together to prepare fall crops for sale.

markets now bring locally grown food directly to the customer. The family is reconsidering operating the stand seven days a week to save time and money. Surrounding the building, the road-front acres are planted in succession with seasonal crops: okra, broccoli, tomatoes, flowers, pumpkins, and squash. As one crop matures and is harvested, the long rows take on new residents. With irrigation added a few years ago, these fields are the Birds' most productive.

The high tunnels, clustered with two greenhouses, are set back from the front acres and the market stand. The long houses have proven to be successful for controlling pests, disease, and the weather. Bird's Haven now sells tomatoes in early May. "We used to plant in May, now we're selling in May," Lee said. He loves the variety of vegetables they produce; with berries and flowers, they plant over 60 different crops in a season. He and his wife, Lindsey, have four children. He's sensitive to the importance of eating real food, food fresh and local, both for his family and others. "Kids need to grow up knowing where their food comes from," he said with a nod to the larger community. The interest in local food nationally segues with the family's personal and business interests and goals. "As long as that interest continues, we will keep growing food," he said.

As the family scales up their endeavor by increasing the scope of production and distribution, they are buffeted by new complexities that can compromise expansion. Little issues can become big issues. Deer and raccoons and groundhogs eat corn and cucumbers, Lee said, not with disgust in his voice, but with quiet resignation that nature is controllable only to a point. He learns to compensate and strategize. "We'll never plant cucumbers in the field again," Lee said. "In the high tunnels, we are yielding more from two rows of cucumbers than we did with 2,000 plants in the field."

With seasonal crops, Lee accepts that part of the harvest will be lost. Fencing robust enough to deter deer and ground-hogs, central Ohio's two hungriest visitors to gardens and fields, is an expensive option and spraying synthetic pesticides for plant pests and diseases conflicts with their desire to be chemical free. Bird's Haven Farms isn't a certified organic operation. The family built their business from the ground up over time and as standards for organic growing expanded over the past decade, they realized compliance was unlikely. "Our high tunnels have treated wood baseboards and you can't have those to be certified. We can't afford to replace them." Lee said, always aware of the lack of capital for farmers growing food. But the basic principles and goals of organic growing are important to Lee and the family. Customers sometimes ask about spraying and chemical use, he said, and Lee is honest in his reply. "We are practicing good growing," he said. When essential, they will only use spray that is zero post harvest. In other words, a spray that leaves no residue. Even organic growers spray when necessary, but they use sprays that are naturally occurring substances, not synthetic. Copper, for example, prevents late blight in tomatoes, a disease that can wipe out an entire field overnight. "Unless we see signs of early or late blight on tomatoes," Tom said, "we won't spray at all."

"People who ask mostly want to know that we grow what we sell," Lee said noting the customer base in Granville is educated and informed, valuing quality over price more often than not. But as the farm increases production by covering more acreage with high tunnels and other methods, the Birds are looking to new, more diverse markets. Buying local at farmers markets isn't enough, he said. "We are growing more than we sell at the farmers markets right now," Lee said, "so we are looking for other ways to move the produce."

∽

Access to markets and access to capital are the new challenges for farms like Bird's Haven, farms now able to produce higher volumes. Until a broader regional or statewide system for collecting and distributing locally grown food to designated markets is in place, Community Supported Agriculture, or CSAs, give the Birds and other growers their best opportunity to increase production. "CSAs have saved the farm," Tom said. Each year, the farm is able to increase the number of shares offered and now offers nearly 300 CSA shares both summer and fall. As the name implies, CSAs are customer's upfront investments in local farmers.

By buying a share of what the farm grows, families invest in the farmer. Their support helps the farmer buy seed, hire labor, and meet the early costs of starting the season. Shares small, medium, or large of this promised market are sold in the early spring for designated amounts of whatever is growing during the high season. When lettuce, pea shoots, and spinach are ready for harvest, for example, a box with various amounts of those vegetables is the week's share. Next week, radishes may be available as the pea shoots finish. Beets and kale may come on next. Each box is a bounty of fresh produce. Shareholders either drive to the farm to pick up their share or farmers provide a pickup location. Bird's Haven Farms offers three pickup points in the Granville area, for example, including the farm and the farmers markets they attend. In late summer, shares for fall CSAs are sold, offering fresh produce well into the waning months of the calendar year.

"CSAs have become a powerful force over the last 10–15 years. They haven't topped out yet for us," he said. "There's just so much demand for local food. We aren't even touching that demand." CSAs provide 60% of the farm's income.

The Birds continue to expand the scope of their CSA by networking with other area farmers and offering their products, such as honey, beef, pork, and goat cheese as options to the weekly share. In addition, Ann's flock of 150 chickens sets her up as a local egg producer. Known fondly as the "egg lady," Ann happily gathers, cleans, and delivers eggs weekly to her customers. These collaborations are good for everyone, producer and customer alike.

To target other markets, Lee and Bryn have made connections with restaurants, small grocery stores, and institutions such as schools and businesses. "The difficulty with restaurants and grocery stores," Bryn said, "is that they often want larger quantities than we can or want to grow. One store the farm sells to would like 600 pints of cherry tomatoes, she said, citing this example. "We can't grow that much without becoming a monoculture farm, but if we can aggregate farmers so each grows 200 pints then together we can meet that demand," she said. "I've seen the result of when farms come together, they may be close to failing on their own, but are stronger when they work together."

Creative networking, getting growers together for mutual benefit, is at the heart of the food hub concept, a regional collection and distribution location where farmers can take their produce for broader distribution. From there, it is either sold in a farmers market or distributed to restaurants or grocery stores. If a local food culture is to ever override the modern, mass-produced integrated system that dominates the country's food production, Bryn said regional food hubs are key. A network of food hubs in Ohio would broaden distribution. "It has to be easy to move food," she said. She managed a food hub in Norfolk, North Carolina, before moving back to the farm to help her brother. "I loved the people interaction there," she said. "It built community for me. I knew everybody, learned their life's stories and saw how local food can really make a difference."

When a community grows up around a food hub and local food is available on an ongoing basis, the new food culture can be sustained, she believes, and spread to all economic segments of a community. Already, many farmers markets accept Supplemental Nutrition Assistance Program (SNAP) benefit cards, the debit card replacement for food stamps. When Bryn returned to her hometown a year ago, she and others also interested in expanding distribution opportunities came together to organize a food hub in Columbus. "I know the only way to make a living from growing food, for me and others, is to start aggregation, to develop the infrastructure for growers to sell in to. I am working towards this selfishly, I suppose, because I want our farm to succeed. I want my brother to make a living. I want my parents to be able to retire. But it also interests me because I want all of these farmers to succeed in an environment that doesn't necessarily support them right now. And I come to this from the producer level."

Bryn encounters lots of growers who would love to ramp up production if they knew the market was there. A food hub gives them that reassurance. "But if there's no promised marketplace, they're not going to be able to grow. Commodity farmers, in particular, will never go from corn and soybeans to food crops without it, she believes. They don't want to do farmers markets and CSAs, that's a pain," she said. "As it is now, they can just drive their crop down to the grain mill and then it's over."

"If we can make it easy and profitable then some might begin to change over. We do the marketing and all of that and they just drive to our warehouse." But Bryn understands this gets political. "A building that would have been a great location was sold out from under us because we were all tied up in sorting out different views about how to do it. We have ideas from the producer level; people with money to invest wanted it a different way."

For Bird's Haven and a few other local growers and producers, Granville's Farm to School program is one success story of collaboration and market expansion in Licking County. Four years ago, Chuck Dilbone retired as Granville's high school principal and turned his time and efforts to establishing a program to improve school lunches by establishing the Farm to School program in the district. This program is part of a national Farm to School program for schools K-12 to connect with local farmers. Eight regional lead agencies offer technical assistance, training, information services, and networking and support for policy, media, and marketing matters. They have participants in all 50 states.

For Dilbone, the program is about good, local food and about cooking. He brought in a chef and a sous chef, and continually develops connections to buy as much local food as he can find. Dilbone, himself, is a farmer, owning Sunbeam Farms, a family produce farm in the Granville area operated by Dilbone's son, Ben, that sells at farmers markets and is in a similar position as Bird's Haven in looking for new markets. The farm is currently moving through the process to become USDA certified organic. So Chuck knows the difference real food can make. He credits support from the school board and parents for the success of the program.

Formerly, the 2,500 students in the district could choose to eat "the school lunch," the potato puff and Sloppy Joe type lunches we all remember. "If they ate lunch at all," Chuck said. Granville schools, like many districts, had stopped cooking lunches. Cooking was outsourced. Lunches prepared early in the day by the large adjoining district, Newark City Schools, were delivered hours later. Fewer than 25% of the Granville students ate the school lunch. Today, 70% of the students eat the school lunch daily, Dilbone says, representing a 38% increase in participation. "The program is really based on cooking," he added. Chuck is invited to share the story of Granville's Farm to School program with districts elsewhere in the state and school representatives visit to see it in action. The program runs with the economic attitude of a restaurant, Dilbone says. "We want trained people to cook real food for kids," he said. Even though the school year doesn't really sync with the growing season, the high tunnels on Bird's Haven Farm, for example, gave the district lettuce until January last year and picked up again in April.

Bryn is cautiously optimistic. With the grass roots efforts she sees all across the state, she believes a meaningful base can develop. "Building the consumer and producer ends drives the infrastructure," she said. "If producers can grow 500 acres of food, we can feed 3,000 people." She, like other advocates, dismisses the contention from agribusiness that local food production could never feed the population. As production increases and markets open up, she is convinced a network of food hubs can be significant.

But until a regional distribution system can ramp up, the Birds rely on CSAs and farm markets. "We started a CSA at Denison and hoped to sign up 20 people," Lee said. "We got 30 right away and had to close it off at that number." With that level of interest and a contract with the local public school for their Farm to School program, in addition to their normal distribution activity, the Birds have so far been able to sell the volume they are producing.

By ramping up production, however, the family may be facing their largest and most perplexing problem: labor. Despite an economic environment of high unemployment, the Birds, like farms everywhere, struggle with finding and keeping employees. Hot days, muddy fields, and long hours are routine on produce farms and despite the desire to be employed, people just don't want to work very hard, Tom said. "Dairy farms have begun to use migrant workers; orchards around here use migrant workers. We may want to as well," he said. "We just can't find anyone local who wants to work."

Lee added, "We want to find people who are as passionate about growing local food as we are and who will stick it out the whole season." But he acknowledges that the wages are low and people get burnt out. Three full time workers and a part-time worker or two gets them through the season right now, Lee said, but there is a lot of rehiring along the way that saps valuable time for the busy farming family. They are exploring alternatives to traditional hiring, such as student interns and immigrant workers. Unlike migrant workers, legal immigrant workers will become local residents and Tom believes this will make them reliable season to season. "It would give us the chance to employ people year round," he said.

When Bryn returned to Ohio, she came as an outreach field coordinator for Rural Coalition out of Washington, D.C. She works in Columbus from office space she rents from Local Matters, a non-profit organization working for systematic change in Ohio's food system. Their mission, as they write it, is "to transform the food system in central Ohio to be more secure, prosperous, just and delicious." Through their association, Bryn is also able to network with others who share her goals. And since her work for Rural Coalition is primarily with minority farmers, she is in touch with the immigrant labor market. She hopes that combination will help her family's farm.

She was invited to speak recently on National Public Radio about the risks and the unpredictability produce farmers face when the weather or some other factor sweeps in and takes an entire crop with it. That interview gained her a spot as a panelist on the Chris Hayes program on MSNBC a few weeks later and gave her the unique opportunity to talk about the challenges of being a local food producer. Commodity farmers receive crop insurance from the government to protect them against weather disasters, she explained. Specialty crop farmers don't. Just this year, Bird's Haven lost $40,000 in sweet corn when the entire crop succumbed to drought. They replanted three times.

"At some point, you have to decide if you can make a profit and make a living," her father Tom said. "Everyone thinks they can start growing food but then the reality sets in that it's lots of long, hard work with no guarantees. At the busy farmers markets, everyone happily makes a little bit of money, but still for most of them, it's a hobby. That's a huge difference from us."

"We're at the point where we're going to break over the top. We either need to dive into this or scale back, maybe just work with the high tunnels and do what we can do. We need to think about how big we want to be."

Sidebar 4

The Economics of Local Food

In his 2011 report on *Ohio's Food Systems*, researcher Ken Meter discusses the impacts of Ohio's food economy on the economic well being of rural Ohio. He concludes that, even though Ohio is an agriculturally productive region, there is a significant net outflow of food dollars. On the income side, Ohio farmers took in about $8.8 billion in commodity sales in 2008. Since 2000 the yearly total has ranged between $6 and $10 billion depending on weather conditions and commodity prices. Even though prices for food have risen substantially, the value of Ohio farm production has actually fallen about 30% since the 1970s. Both livestock and milk sales declined significantly as these industries have consolidated. On the expenditure side, Ohioans now purchase about $29 billion of food per year, $17 billion for home consumption and $12 billion dining out.

Because sizeable fractions of farm inputs (about $4 billion) as well as up to 85% of fresh and prepared foods are sourced out of state, Meter concludes that Ohio sees a net outflow of some $30 billion food dollars annually. Dollars, that if re-circulated within local economies, could have a large impact on jobs and incomes as well as economic resilience or stability. Meter estimates that if local food purchases increased to 15% of Ohioans' food budget, it would bring an additional $2.5 billion in farm income, almost a 33% increase. Where and on what the money is spent is important. Research by the British New Economics Foundation indicates that money spent at local farmers markets has twice the multiplier effect of money spent at local supermarkets, meaning the money is circulated in the local economy more rapidly and for a longer period of time before it leaks out through external purchases or investments. While we clearly live in a global economy, Meter and many others conclude that local food expenditures bring the greatest economic benefits to an area.

There are numerous direct and indirect impediments to expanding local food production and consumption including legal hurdles, government subsidies, infrastructure constraints, credit availability, and, of course, consumer demand for local food. From the farmer's perspective having stable markets is the central concern. Given the range of environmental and pricing uncertainties that they face, farmers need to be certain of reliable markets before embarking on new investments to expand and diversify production.

Market opportunities for local farm products include on-farm sales, farmers markets, CSAs (both individual and institutional), local groceries and supermarkets, institutional buyers, and local food cooperatives. Farmers in this collection of stories discuss many of these avenues. On-farm sales do not and probably should not account for a large fraction of direct sales given numerous inherent inefficiencies from farmers' time spent managing roadside stands to consumers driving long distances for uncertain purchases. Farmers markets continue to grow nationally but in places, particularly the northeastern U.S., appear to be nearing saturation. CSAs have many advantages for the farmer, particularly financial because payments are made at the beginning of the growing season when input costs are highest and because the weekly food basket can be adjusted based on the vagaries of the weather and yields of various crops. For local foods sales to increase substantially beyond the present 2% of food purchases, though, larger stable markets must be established to warrant a significant expansion of food production.

Unlike mechanized commodity crop production, expanded production of local foods will require more labor. Some increase could come from the adaptable small farms and gardens that currently supply much of the local market. For production to increase substantially either more small farms will need to be established or larger farms that now focus on straight conventional agriculture will need to diversify. This second path is complicated by the large debt load, from both land and equipment, that most commodity farmers currently carry. They also may not have the time to face the steep learning curve required to move into new modes of production, as exemplified by the Bird's Haven Farm operation. In either case though, farmers, viewed collectively, as well as rural communities do stand to gain from the added value of fresh produce compared to commodity products.

Large institutional buyers can provide stable long-term markets to promote expansion of agricultural investment and can serve as catalysts for further demand and production. The Granville Exempted Village Schools' rapidly growing four-year-old Farm to School program has gained notoriety for serving healthy meals prepared on-site using raw, organic ingredients at a minimal increase in cost. According to Chuck Dilbone, Director of Business Operations, stable markets for producers are being developed as about 23% of the 2011–2012 annual food budget of $335,000 is sourced within 100 miles of the school with a goal of 45% within 50 miles within 1–2 years. Unfortunately, the educational season and growing season are not well aligned. Some products like apples and potatoes can be effectively stored, and hoop houses and high tunnels allow farmers to expand the season for fresh vegetables up to two months in the spring and fall. But to some degree the school must adjust its menu to the season.

Beginning in the spring of 2013, Denison University, a residential liberal arts college of 2100 students located in Granville, is investing heavily to renovate and expand kitchen facilities to allow for on site preparation and storage of foods coming directly from local farms. The many steps from raw food to prepared dishes will become much more visible serving both to educate and assure students about food quality. Niles Gebele, General Manager of Denison Dining Services operated by Sodexo, states that local farms are supplying many vegetables and much of the college's beef is raised on a farm bordering Denison. Local chicken and pork sources are being developed. Presently about 21% of food purchases are sourced within 150 miles of campus.

The push for local foods continues to spread. Luke Messinger, the Director of Dawes Arboretum south of Newark, is pressing local caterers to use local foods as much as possible for the 200+ weddings at the arboretum each year. The arboretum is also developing an interactive farm display to educate the public about the importance of local food production.

In neighboring Knox County, Kenyon College, another liberal arts college somewhat smaller than Denison, and their food supplier AVI Foodsystems, lead the local food transition in central Ohio by bringing fresh, high-quality local food to students, decreasing environmental impacts, and increasing the college's positive contributions to the local economy. Damon Remillard, AVI Resident Director, states that in 2011–2012 the college spent about $650,000 (40% of the food budget) on local food purchases, including all eggs, milk, pork, beef, potatoes, apples, and honey as well as considerable cheese, sweet corn, and organic grains. The college seeks to promote a stable agricultural community to maintain the rural character of the region. Thus, purchasing efforts are holistic focusing not only on the proximity of suppliers, favoring farms within 25 miles when possible, but supporting family-scale farming, and particularly building stable long-term relationships with producers.

The Kenyon experience illustrates the many positive linkages that develop when buying local. The college has helped farmers with investments, such as high tunnels to lengthen the production season. Linked to their *Food for Thought* curriculum, students volunteer their labor during critical harvest periods. With a stable market and particularly a more stable price structure, farmers and processors are investing to expand production. According to Howard Sacks, Kenyon sociology professor, college initiatives are bringing wider benefits. Kenyon helped develop the Knox County Local Food Council, which has helped to establish local farmers markets in every incorporated town in the county. The county hospital, in conjunction with AVI, is now increasing local food purchases as are numerous restaurants. Plans are underway to establish a year round market in Mount Vernon, the county seat. Remillard believes the next critical step toward a truly stable, integrated farm-to-consumer food system is the development of appropriately-scaled processing and storage facilities such as flash freezing and packaging, the same sort of strategies the Birds are working on through their advocacy.

— Tod Frolking

Chapter 5

Do the Right Thing

Organic farming appealed to me because it involved searching for and discovering nature's pathways, as opposed to the formulaic approach of chemical farming. The appeal of organic farming is boundless; this mountain has no top, this river has no end.

— Eliot Coleman
The New Organic Grower, 1989

During my childhood on the farm, the word "organic" as it applied to growing food wasn't part of any conversation I remember ever hearing. Food resulted when you dropped a seed into the soil and it grew. Simple. But something was stealthily happening on our neighboring farms and elsewhere across the state and the country that would change the course of the American diet, a generational shift so invasive it helped spark modern environmentalism and now, fuels a changing food culture. Since then, the word "organic" has gone from perhaps its first appearance as the "crunchy granola" demographic to mainstream America. As might be expected, the word has become branded, by repetition if nothing else.

Laura and Mike Laughlin, growers of certified organic produce at their Northridge Organic Farm, spend their Saturdays together at the Worthington farmers market.

But under that brand, the local food movement can be better understood.

Conventional thinking held that new powerful synthetic pesticides sprayed and dusted on fields far and wide in this mid-20th-Century America was the magic bullet to manage insect damage and plant disease. This killing deftly targeted the worst of the offenders, but it also affected non-targeted organisms, sifted into the soil, and lingered in the air. Farmers like Wib and Charley, or our neighbors to the west, Dan and Mose, began to realize increased crop production with these new aids. To add to this arsenal, synthetic fertilizers came on line at about the same time and the number of acres planted grew along with the crops. It must have been exciting to them then to watch their production numbers, and their income, rise. It all seemed charmed.

Those who work the soil are always looking for ways to cooperate with Mother Nature, or as human nature has it, to control the natural systems of the earth. From old farm garden remedies like attracting slugs to a drowning death with saucers of beer to more sustainable practices like maintaining diversity by planting a variety of crops to keep those bugs guessing, farmers have discovered strategies over time that work, sometimes. But when synthetic chemical substances hit the market during what is called the "pesticide era" of post World War II, the skirmishes got serious. The EPA reports that in 2006 and 2007, for example, the U.S. used approximately 1.1 billion pounds of pesticides on crops, 22% of the world's total. As organisms gradually adapt to synthetic inputs, the inputs must get stronger. It's a dangerous cycle and, really, one can't imagine Mother Nature losing.

A small minority of gardeners and farmers, just a handful at first, resisted the popular use of these chemical wonders. Mike and Laura Laughlin, backyard gardeners who became organic produce farmers, are among them. "To me, it just makes sense to grow naturally," Mike said. "I want good clean healthy food for myself and my family. And when I started growing on a larger scale, I couldn't see a way to produce anything else and sell it to other families. It wouldn't be right." For Mike, organic growing is about growing food that does no harm.

Mike and Laura went from a flourishing backyard garden in their urban home in Columbus to 20 acres in rural Licking County where conventional farms surround them. When they moved to their new land in 1994, they planted their first garden that next spring. The future Northridge Organic Farm was born, but it would take several years before the word "organic" rang true. That part of the story is to come.

The Laughlins are vegetable growers and they were excited to try their hand at growing naturally on a larger scale than their backyard garden permitted. Their early gardening produced enough for their own family and enough excess to dabble in small local farmers markets, just beginning to crop up in central Ohio. They liked being part of the community at the market, getting to know their customers who stopped by week after week and their fellow vendors with whom they shared stories and advice, and they liked watching people walk away carrying the good tasting healthy food they grow.

On their new land, they could grow so much more. "We planted part of the front field, three quarters of an acre or so,"

Mike said as he talked about that first year. He and Laura, a nurse, were both working day jobs then and commuting to Columbus, about 30 miles away. "We'd get home about 4 and work until dark to make deliveries the next morning, then go to work and start all over again," Laura said.

Their front field garden grew to more than an acre and then they prepared another two-acre field behind the house. Then, as they expanded, they began to till and plant other, more distant parts of their acreage. Farther down a deeply rutted farm road that passes a greenhouse and farm building, then crosses a busy stream and twists and turns through a wooded area, the land opens again to long, wide fields where two high tunnels sit before carefully etched out plots of vegetables. One of those plots is planted with 7,000 heirloom tomato plants.

"It's our specialty crop," Mike says. Like many small-scale vegetable farmers in the state, they know that Ohioans love tomatoes, flavor-rich fruits high in nutritional value. In fact, the tomato is the state's largest vegetable crop. Heirlooms, or "antique" varieties nearly lost because they are generally unsuitable for the long distances food must travel from farm to market in an agribusiness environment, are strong sellers at farmers markets and to restaurants, and are popular among farmers market producers. They come in all sorts of colorful shapes and sizes, for example, the dark flesh of the Cherokee Purple to the pinkish red of the beefy Crinkovic, or the tangy taste of Aunt Ruby's German Green.

Their personal favorite is a family heirloom of their own, Grandpa Nick's Roma style tomato. "It's a large, paste variety with a sweet flavor," said Mike. "We make all our sauces with

Each variety of vegetable at the Laughlin's market stand is identified by name. Customers come to know those names and return week after week looking for their favorite varieties.

this tomato and it's a big seller at the markets." When Laura's grandfather emigrated to the United States from Italy in the early 1900s, he brought along seeds for the tomato he'd been growing and using for years. Each year, he would save the seeds from the latest crop. Members of Laura's family gradually began planting the fruit and saving the seeds themselves. "It's a bit fussy to grow," Laura said, "but everyone loves it." Under the careful stewardship of seed savers who have kept varieties of tomatoes and other vegetables alive despite the crush of a monoculture environment of conventional food production, and through gardeners like Laura and Mike who value diversity in the botanical world, people are discovering a vast assortment of squash, melons, cucumbers, and tomatoes at their farmers markets that they never knew existed. Mike and Laura grow 60 different varieties of heirloom tomatoes. And, except for what they keep for their own use, they sell every tomato they grow.

The farm grows a harvest basket of vegetables, in fact. Twenty to thirty different kinds of lettuces and greens like mustard and kale, and several varieties of onions, radishes, summer squash, and eggplant stretch green down long rows. "We like to grow kind of outside the box," he said. "For example, we grow potatoes, but not the white Russets you find in the stores, but red skins and those with blue flesh or pink flesh. And lots of sweet potatoes. So much of the time, you get benign fiber in store potatoes. There's not a lot of flavor or nutrition left," he said, referring to potatoes and other vegetables grown more for their ability to withstand long shipping journeys than their flavor or nutrition. "We stay away from that, we're not competing with those sorts of potatoes."

This season, Mike hopes to dig and harvest 25,000 – 30,000 pounds of potatoes, "if I can keep the deer out of them," he says.

∽

So in those early years as the Laughlins planted vegetables and worked on building soil weakened by conventional farming practices, they were pretty much working in isolation. No one around them grew naturally, much less organically.

"A long time ago, the mid-1980s, I got involved with a brand new little group called OEFFA," Mike said, referring to the Ohio Ecological Farm and Food Association, headquartered in Columbus. "I went to a conference, just their third one or so, and remember walking into this room where a speaker was talking about organic farming. There must have been 150 people there, it was just incredible," he said.

Affirmed and excited about meeting and talking with other organic growers, he joined the organization, established in 1979 as a "grassroots coalition of farmers, backyard gardeners, consumers, retailers, educators, researchers, and others who share a desire to build a healthy food system." The organization aims to preserve farmland, promote food security for all Ohioans and create economic opportunities for rural communities. Coincidentally, its executive director lives in Granville.

In 1990, the Organic Foods Production Act established the National Organic Program and the development of national standards followed. OEFFA was among the first certifiers to be accredited by the USDA and remains Ohio's largest certifier. By October 2002, all organic farmers, processors, handlers, and certifiers had to be in compliance with regulations over production, handling, and labeling if their goal was to grow and sell USDA Organic. With that stamp of certification, producers can sell their produce at higher prices, a trend that continues today with the popularity of the brand.

Mike chaired the organic certification process for Ohio in those start up years. "We first started with just a handful, maybe 12 certified organic farms," he said. "Now we have about 700. Somewhere in my archives I still have that first certification form. It was one piece of paper with the standards on one side and the application on the other," he said. "Now the standards are like a telephone book."

Mike's involvement with OEFFA gave him confidence. "Seeing what I saw there," he said, "I could just see that there was a need and a place for this. So we slowly, but surely, worked at trying different techniques in our backyard garden, techniques that we transferred to a larger scale when we bought the farm." Achieving certification that would enable them to declare their produce organic and sell it under the USDA organic seal didn't come easily or quickly. "Lots of people thought we were just plain nuts," Laura said. "We felt ridiculed at times, but we were just regular people, we weren't out there tooting our own horn at all."

Neighbors who were conventional farmers raised their eyebrows, Mike said, when the new Northridge Organic Farm moved in. "I know they thought we were coming in here to tell them what to do, but I made it clear from the beginning that I know you're just trying to make a living the best you can and I'm not here to tell you what to do."

But a more pressing challenge than the reactions of their neighbors was the condition of the soil on their land. "The land had been farmed conventionally, but not for a long time," Mike said. "But it had been abused with chemicals and overproduction. So we've spent years, we're still working on it, putting lots of organic matter back into the soil through composting crops, letting sheep graze on it, soil testing to know what minerals need to be added back in to balance it out. You have to understand the chemistry of the soil to amend it accordingly."

"Growing organically has been a constant educational process," Mike said. "What is good healthy food and what does it mean to you? How do you get the flavors? It all starts with the soil. It not only has to be balanced nutritionally, but the whole ecosystem has to be working, all the microorganisms and the worms working to make the nutrients available to the plants. That's what makes a tomato taste good. To me, it all makes perfect sense."

The first piece in gaining organic certification is, in fact, the land. "It has to be free of synthetic influence for three years prior to harvest," he said. "Until then, you can grow on it and sell your produce, but you can't call it certified organic." Mike and Laura were able to accelerate the process of their own certification some by getting signed affidavits from neighbors that the land here hadn't been farmed for at least six years. With certification then in hand, the Laughlins launched Northridge Organic Farm.

∿

As the volume and the quality of their produce grew, so did their reputation. Mike and Laura do three farmers markets each week: Wednesday, Thursday, and Saturday, May through October. With four seasonal employees now, they are constantly digging onions, picking beans, cutting lettuce, and harvesting vegetables as they come to maturity, spending the entire day before market preparing: getting up in the wee hours, getting there, and setting up…it's a busy lifestyle, Mike says, but they love it. "When you're putting that food in a person's hands and they come back and tell you what they thought of it, well, we just make great friendships. When the markets end in October, it's kind of sad. We miss the people over the winter," he said, but added, with a pause, "But we don't miss all the work that goes into it."

Because of the high standards for operation and the time needed to qualify for certification, usually only a handful of farmers at farmers markets can sell under the USDA organic symbol, a label that has come to give public assurance of growing practice. That number is growing, however, as farms recognize the level of comfort "USDA Organic" brings to customers and serves to increase demand. They gradually work towards certification. Another farm in the area is in year two of the three-year waiting period for the land to be considered clean. They are looking forward to the day they can label the good food they already grow "organic." Mike is comfortable with the standards for growing set by the National Organic Program. He's been growing organically since his first garden and he says nothing that comes his way is a surprise or a handicap. "The hardest thing, I guess," he says, "is the record keeping for traceability. We keep track of the harvest on a daily basis with a field log. Then once the food is packed and sold, we keep records of the sales. The harvest needs to balance the sales. All of these numbers are transferred from the field logs to the computer. That takes a lot of time." Yearly, a representative of OEFFA visits the farm, tours the fields, and checks the records.

Their organic label at farmers markets gives the Laughlins recognition and brings attention to their food. With varietal labeling and through conversation with customers, they are also deliberately working to brand their name. These are challenging, but important areas that small-scale farmers often lack experience with, Mike says. But he has a process. "We just don't put out radishes or eggplant. We identify the varieties and label them. Clara, for example, is a large white Italian hybrid eggplant that matures early. You put the name on it, customers buy it and like it and they come back the next week to us looking for that variety."

The Laughlins have witnessed first hand the growth of the food movement through the phenomenal growth of farmers markets. "When we started, there would be maybe 15 farmers. We would visit with everybody. Now it's so busy, it takes both of us and we barely get a chance to leave the table. The demand for good local food is so strong."

Northridge Organic Farm, unlike many specialty crop farms looking to widen distribution, doesn't do CSAs. By coincidence perhaps, they say their visibility at the markets attracted the attention, for example, of the chef at the Worthington Inn, a high end Columbus restaurant. He started buying their tomatoes, lettuce, and other vegetables for as long as the growing season permitted. More restaurants followed. Then they were approached by the owners of a new concept restaurant that would celebrate local food by not only using it, but also by telling customers about it, including where it comes from. The Northstar Café, first opened in 2004 and now in four locations in Columbus, buys as much local food as it can, some of it from Northridge. It's part of their mission statement. "They want quality across the board and they advertise that," Mike said. "There was really no one then doing that kind of quality. We've been with them since they opened." Northstar buys their heirloom tomatoes, lettuce, and sweet potatoes throughout the season, which the farm can extend now with high tunnel growing. "We start in April and sell to them through October," Laura said. "Or longer, we're only down a few months. But by the end of the season, the restaurants they serve are only getting a few things as the season winds down. We really do try to push eating seasonally and some of the restaurants we work with change their menus to reflect the season, or they create specials that make use of our fresh products."

Northridge Organic Farm also sells to a few wholesalers who distribute to stores and other restaurants, such as Green Bean Delivery in Columbus, a for-profit organization that operates like a CSA. "This is good for us financially and easy, allowing us to move excess produce if we have it. We're growing to meet demand though and aren't going to have a lot of excess." They can deliver as much as 5,000 pounds a week to wholesalers and other retail locations.

The Laughlins are full time produce farmers and make a living from their farm now. "It's taken years," Laura said. "The demand for what we grow has skyrocketed in the last five years and we now know what we're doing, so it's a combination of things. A lot of trial and error."

A few years ago, they hired their first employees and bought some machinery, most of it used. These two things, Laura said, took them from large-scale gardening to small-scale farming and made a tremendous difference in what they could produce. "That giant leap was important, but scary at the time," she said.

They're excited about what's happening with local food in Ohio. "If you look at the demographics, where the population centers are, central Ohio is a hot spot," Mike said. Can this be a sign of sustainability in the local food market? Not yet, Mike says. People don't really realize yet the real cost of cheap food. "There's still a wall," he said. "We talk about the health and obesity issues all the time," he said, but people still complain about the cost of food and still look for the cheapest tomato regardless of how bad it tastes. "One of my favorite things to say to the complainers is to invite them to the farm. 'We'd love to have you come out and see what we do,' I tell them."

As much as changing cultural attitudes, Mike, like others in these stories, sees the pressing need to address the supply and distribution issues in Ohio. "We just don't have enough growers to meet the demand now. From our perspective, farmers markets are growing by 15–20% a year just from what we sell. It's phenomenal. The problem is there's just not enough farmers to go around or not enough conventional farmers yet willing to change over."

Mike and Laura don't want to get bigger though. "I don't want to buy a 200-acre farm and increase the yield to meet the demand. I'd rather see four or five younger farmers get started. It really makes sense to have 20 smaller farmers meet the demand. You definitely work hard, but you can now make a decent living and you're doing your part in starting that rural economy back up. Where those 20 farmers buy equipment and supplies, they're supporting other local businesses, then they're hiring people from the community, and it just goes on. That's what I'd like to see us do."

Every now and then in the earlier years, Mike and Laura would put up a booth at the Farm Science Review in Columbus. "We were like the leper colony," Mike remembers now with a glint of amusement. People would walk on the opposite side of the aisle to get past our booth. Then we noticed they were starting to walk closer and after a few years, some stopped and asked questions. "The best way to have an impact is to just keep doing what you know in your heart is right. If another person realizes that and another, it's growing, maybe slowly, but it's a sustainable growth. That's the only way."

Sidebar 5

What's with the Silt?

From an agricultural perspective, a key aspect of a soil is the particle size distribution of its mineral grains. Soils are classified according to the percentage of sand, silt, and clay, collectively called the fine fraction. Everyone has heard of clay and sand. Clay, in fact, becomes almost a generic label for Ohio soil. Silt, a term uncommon to most, certainly gets the short shrift. Most who rub soil between their fingers and notice that it lacks gritty sand will invariably call it "clay," even though the actual clay content may be only 10-20%. In Licking County, where most of the farmers in this collection of stories reside, about 73% of the top soils are actually silt loams, meaning that at least 50% of the soil is silt, less than 28% is clay. The word loam indicates a mixture of the three fine fraction classes. Another 13% of the soils are channery silt loams, that is, silty with an abundance of angular rock fragments derived from local sandstones. This dominance of silt is seen across most of the agricultural heartland of the Midwest and Mississippi alluvial basin. So what's with this under recognized sediment?

Silt is actually easy to identify. If the material isn't strongly cohesive (i.e. clay) and is too fine to feel a graininess (i.e. sand), it is silt. The boundary between sand and silt, 50 to 63 microns depending on the system used, is a practical one. It's the limit of our touch (sensitivity) to feel individual grains. Silt feels like flour. Much of the silt covering the Midwest originates from the Pleistocene ice sheets. As a glacier, with much rock debris imbedded in its basal ice, slides over bedrock, it abrades that surface much like sandpaper and produces rock dust or rock flour. The milky meltwater rivers issuing from the snouts of glaciers are loaded with this pulverized rock. While the bulk of Midwestern silt is quartz, a physically strong and chemically resistant mineral, enough other primary minerals from diverse bedrock to the north and carbonates from abraded limestones are present to add significant fertility to the mixture.

Silt loams provide a great physical environment for plant growth. With some clay and humus present, granular aggregates develop that promote rapid infiltration of water through large pores and at the same time hold a large volume of water available to plants in the fine pores within the aggregates. Sandy soils hold little water and clay soils generally have low permeability and are prone to ponding. While the silt is critical for the soil's physical properties, the clay and organic humus fractions are critical for nutrient retention and exchange.

The waning stage of the last ice age was a dusty time. Broad shallow streams carrying heavy loads of rock flour would dry up during the cold winters and strong winds would blow the silt off the outwash plains and transport it miles downwind spreading the valuable silt, or loess, broadly across the landscape. The soil in the Kale Yard, for example, is the Ockley silt loam, which typically has a 12–16-inch silt cap overlying sandy and gravelly loam. Bird's Haven Farm and Northridge Organic Farm sit mainly on the Centerburg silt loam composed mostly of compact glacial till that is in itself quite silty, but then is mantled by a thin cover of loess. A central reason to try to protect the topsoil in much of Ohio and the Midwest is to maintain this easily eroded silt cap. The underlying glacial tills and bedrock will generally not yield such workable, productive soil material.

— Tod Frolking

Chapter 6

Good Food for All

There must be a better way. Find it!

— Thomas Edison
Poster at Menlo Park, date uncertain

It's a rambunctious time out there on the other side of the picture window at Snowville Creamery. Under the warm sun, rich fertile soil floods grasses with nutrients and energy to send pulsing shoots skyward into the bright light of springtime. As a result, luminous green mounds of tender new grass now blanket the ground, tumbling in the breezes of the season left to right as far as the eye can see through the frame of the window.

Deep in those grassy pastures and up and down gentle valleys of the Appalachian foothills of Southern Ohio, brown cows hold their ground as spring riots on. With heads buried up to their ears, they search out their favorites among the sweet new grasses. Cows within eye range of the low slung building take no note of the window or of those of us who gaze through it. They are fully committed to the grass.

Farther away on a ridge top is a small paddock, a blotch of brown framed in green. There a small cluster of cows await

◀ Warren and Victoria Taylor's Snowville Creamery is an on-the-farm dairy, processing and packaging milk for local distribution from grass-grazed cows.

the imminent birth of their calves and then, finally, for their turn on the grass. It's the start of a season of freshness in more ways than one. In dairy language, a cow lactates or becomes fresh each year when she gives birth, ready for a season of daily milking, morning and night. And if she lives on this farm, she will enjoy a gentle, quiet life on the grass in between.

On the other side of the window, Saturday milk production at Snowville Creamery is underway. Every Tuesday, Thursday, and Saturday, fresh milk from the brown cows just outside the window is packaged for local distribution. Today, soft swishing sounds of milk whisking through miles of snaking stainless steel pipes behind the closed doors of the production room catch my attention. In this room, the picture window room, however, fingers quietly tap keyboards, and a handful of young men and women talk and laugh as they go about their work. One voice among those in the creamery is the voice they listen to. It belongs to Warren Taylor, who along with his wife, Victoria, raised Snowville Creamery up on the same grassy pasture it now shares with 250 brown cows.

Warren is the consummate dairyman from a family of dairymen. His passion for making affordable high-value milk for local distribution guides his every action and decision. He regularly works 100-hour weeks, Victoria says. He is always and sometimes dairyman, founder, promoter, salesman, lobbyist, mechanic, engineer, delivery driver, and decision maker. "Cut me and I bleed white," he says with a smile on his face.

Grass engulfs Warren and his creamery. He likes it that way. For him, the grass holds everything critical to making good milk. On the grass, cows live a natural life as ruminants.

With digestive systems that allow them to process leafy plant material that is indigestible to humans and then to regurgitate and re-chew the "cud," they are meant to roam green fields all day long. On the grass, the flavor and quality of the milk they produce is at its nutritional best, Warren says. And then from the grass, the milk these cows make gets into the bellies of local children and their families as fast as Warren can package and deliver it.

The modest 6,000-square-foot plant constructed in 2005 of recycled materials sits on one acre of a 280-acre dairy farm owned by Bill Dix and Stacy Hall outside of the town of Pomeroy, deep in southeast Ohio. The cows are milked every day just 100 yards from the door of the plant. And with the most minimal pasteurizing the law permits — heating milk below 170 degrees for about 20 seconds to kill microorganisms that could cause disease or spoilage — the integrity of flavor and nutrition is preserved. "It's milk the way it used to be," Warren says. Snowville milk is not homogenized either, or mixed to emulsify and disperse the fat content. This allows the buttery yellow cream to naturally rise to the top, a feature most Americans have never seen before. "Shake gently before using," advises the signature green-and-white half-gallon milk cartons where a bold woodcut image of a dairymaid pouring milk from her pail is the Creamery's logo. Snowville's fresh milk goes from cow to carton to customer in less than 48 hours. "It's pure, sweet, and fresh," touts John Stout, the plant manager of this dairy, a Same Day Dairy, Warren dubs it.

Snowville milk in whole milk, two percent, non-fat, chocolate, whipping cream, and half and half is sold locally in neighboring Athens, in select towns like Granville, and in the state's larger cities of Columbus in the center of the state, Cincinnati to the southwest, and Cleveland, the farthest north. In one week, for example, the Creamery produced 19,075 cartons of milk. A line of yogurts is coming soon, Warren says. And the Creamery produces the entire basic product, about 800 gallons a week, for use by Jeni's Splendid Ice Cream, a popular Ohio ice cream artisan. Because the creamery is deep in southeastern Ohio near the state line, Snowville's markets dip into the adjacent states of Kentucky and West Virginia. While the concept of "local food" can be defined by different distances, it is generally considered to be food grown or produced within a radius of thirty to a hundred or so miles, or even a day's drive from its source at most. Snowville is 90 miles from Granville.

Warren believes food should be grown, produced, and distributed locally and he frets over transportation even within the acceptable definition of local miles, a problem he can't yet solve. "We try to minimize our carbon footprint, but then here we are driving a diesel truck to Columbus to deliver milk. When we complain about the cost of food, we're really complaining about the cost of transportation," he said. A convenient coincidence that he lives with, however, happens to take Snowville milk further afield than Warren would ever take it himself. More than 50% of Snowville's milk is purchased by Whole Foods. That milk is on the shelves of every Whole Foods store in Ohio. And because a Whole Foods truck regularly drives within ten miles of the Creamery heading south to the nation's capital city and because Whole Foods recognizes

Snowville's value added product, the milk travels to more than 20 Washington, D.C., area stores as well. "If we had to transport it there, it wouldn't happen," John says, echoing Warren's commitment to reducing the use of fossil fuels to transport food great distances from its source. "We are a local regional business. If we want our milk to be in some other area than we can service locally, then we need to build a plant there." But the Washington market is also strategic. Warren is no stranger to the capital city. He has years of giving testimony under his belt to committees on behalf of the dairy industry, both when he worked in the conventional dairy business and now as an independent dairyman. He has authored articles, written letters, and been the subject of numerous newspaper and magazine articles. NPR radio, for example, interviewed him for a program entitled, "Got (Good) Milk? Ask the Dairy Evangelist." And he's keen to elect local officials who will speak and act for local food economies, even running for office himself at one point. Warren is committed to the long view of bringing good, healthy local milk to the table of every American via a network of local plants supported by local grazing farms. Warren is not a reticent man. He will tell you that for the rest of his life, he's on a crusade.

The big picture window is far more than a window to a scenic view. It certainly seems to have been placed there to remind everyone not to lose sight of the grass, to remember how good the milk is here because of the grass. Warren will quickly tell you that the symbiotic relationship between grass and dairy cow is why Snowville exists and why the creamery may be the best example for the possibilities of establishing a local food movement that works on a broader scale. When critics of the local food movement charge that small-scale production of local food can never feed a large population, Warren and scores of others — farmers, academics, and even some politicians — beg to differ, accusing big agribusiness of trying to snuff out small farmers to secure their hold on the food industry. Warren can tell stories about the battles he's fought with major dairy producers over shelf space in grocery store coolers as one example of power and intent. He can tell you of exorbitant fees and stiff regulations imposed on small dairies and small farmers that he believes are intended to push Snowville and other independent dairies out of the market. He has lots of stories to tell.

The cows on this farm are part of a managed grazing strategy. "Grazing dairy farms commonly grow forage up to knee high and have it promptly eaten down again by grazing cows, many times per year," Warren says. This dairy farm has a network of designated "roadways" to move cattle from pasture to pasture, a costly infrastructure built to protect the grassy hillsides from those crisscrossing cow paths that damage pastures. In some cases, pasture boundaries change in size and location with movable fencing as the grass grows and is consumed. Every day, for example, the cows eat all they want as fast as they want and then they are moved via this network of fenced pathways onto new pastures. The foraged ones re-grow, now with a dose of natural fertilizer, fresh cow manure. A tunnel under the road provides access to other pastures as the cows move easily to new grass, giving them needed exercise, something the majority of dairy cows in this country no longer enjoy. When winter comes and the cows go dry in preparation for their next lacation, their grass diet is supplemented with hay and grain in the winter feeding pad. This wintering over space is a flat graveled area covered with geotextile cloth and more gravel. As the excess hay is moved around by the foraging cows and becomes bedding that accumulates their manure, the pile gets taller and taller. In the spring, the area is bulldozed and the sizable remainder – lots of carbon from the hay and lots of nitrogen from the manure – is spread over the pastures. "It's the main fertility into our farm," Stacy says.

As the grassy pastures on the farm continue to improve year to year, the amount of grain fed declines. "We feed about 10 pounds of grain per day in two meals," Stacy said, "one third corn, one third wheat, and one third wheat middlings, [a by-product of wheat milling that is high in protein and fiber]. Confined cattle, who never eat fresh grass, eat as much as 25 pounds a day plus corn silage." Warren attributes the natural taste of his milk partly to the fact that the Snowville cows don't eat silage, which he says tends to "flavor" the milk.

With a summer grazing diet of fresh grass, Warren says that a cow well adapted to the environment creates rich milk that is a source of two important fatty acids: Omega-3s and Conjugated Linoleic Acids (CLA). As just one example of what happened to milk and other animal and plant products among other changes in agriculture as efficiency and growth took over, John tells the story of how dairy farmers were talked into buying those big blue low oxygen Harvestore silos in the early 1950s for creating silage. Today, the popularity of these

Cows well adapted to their environment and allowed to graze freely on lush pastures create the rich healthy milk that goes into Warren Taylor's Snowville cartons.

expensive glass-fused-to-steel structures has waned, but they still dot the landscape of farms all across the Midwest, especially in Wisconsin, the dairy state, where they became widespread in the 70s. Clustered together, the dark blue projectiles tower over the regular farm silos and dwarf everything in their wake. They seem strangely out of place, stormy blue invaders as they are. When farmers, eager to get a leg up on production, sited these giant towers on their land, they certainly then had to fill them with the silage they were meant to store — grasses, corn stalks, and other organics that ferment into a soupy smelly slurry to supplement the diet of cows taken off the grass and confined in feed lots. Then they had to make enough milk from their dairy herd to pay off the debt. Local lore suggested that the number of Harvestores standing on the farm could measure the success of the dairy farmer. Over time and with other motivators to get big or get out, dairies grew in size. The heavy milking breed, the large black and white Holstein, became favored, replacing the smaller brown Jerseys, Brown Swiss, and Guernseys like Stacy's and Bill's that produce rich, sweet milk, higher in butterfat and protein. Thus, for efficiency and increased yields, cows taken off the grass and confined in tight barns were fed corn-based grain diets along with silage and hay. A confined cow's diet can be 90% corn-based grain. These Confined Animal Feeding Operations (CAFOs) are now synonymous with milk, egg, and meat production. Confinement, however, leads to disease, indigestible corn in ruminants leads to shortened lives, and a cycle of administered hormones and antibiotics began that today characterizes conventional dairies and meat production confinement farms across the country. And, there are the manure lagoons, polluted waterways, and other environmental hazards that result from mass animal confinement.

Now, just 3% of American dairy farms produce more than half of the total volume of milk. In these large industrial confinement farms, cows are raised, milked, and turned into hamburger in an average of four years. "It's a life sentence," Stacy says. Warren also maintains their relatively short life span compromises the quality of milk they can produce. But when a herd of genetically diverse cows are bred and raised generation after generation to adapt to the climate and topography of an area, put on good grass from managed pastures, and allowed to lead long normal diary cow lives Bill, Stacy, and

Warren will tell you that the milk from those cows is "Milk the Way it Used to Be," a phrase that appears on every milk carton leaving the Snowville plant. It's just darn good food that everyone should have a right to drink, Warren says, steel-eyed. He means it.

Warren doesn't mind being called a dairy nerd. In fact, he sports that label and others for the cause of local food and good milk. *Dairy Nerd. Dairy Revolutionary. Dairy Evangelist* – that one's on the back of his business card. When you meet Warren, the titles seem fitting. Tall, lean, with thinning sandy-colored hair and piercing blue eyes, he is so visibly passionate about his small local dairy that he can barely be still. He flushes instantly with mixtures of passion, anger, and excitement as he talks ceaselessly about good milk, pastured cows, government subsidies, agribusiness, transportation, local foods, and yes, even fracking, the drilling for oil and gas which he believes is demonizing the land and threatening to encroach on his county and ruin the water as well as the Appalachia-like lifestyle of southern Ohio. Meigs County is one of the most impoverished counties in the state and landowners have been readily tempted to sell their mineral rights without a second thought. He fumes at that.

When the 52-year-old filler machine that pops open the half-gallon cartons, fills them with milk and seals them goes down (more often than anyone at Snowville would care to think about), Warren races to the rescue, knowing this machinery as well as he knows the milk that flows through it. At 10 A.M. on Saturday, the week's biggest production day, the motor is smoking. Warren hurries in, drops his bag and pushes through the double doors. The filler is the first stainless steel machine inside those doors, last in the sequence of processing and packaging milk. Meanwhile, the humming and swishing of the morning's milk moving through stainless pipes and swirling in tanks waiting to fill hundreds of cartons replaces the sound of the stilled motor. "When the plant is operating, it's a living, breathing organism," he says as he gestures to the stainless steel network. No one seems too distraught or surprised at today's silence though. "I had hoped to go home this morning to work in the garden," John says, but he knows that like other days now and then, that won't happen. He smiles, shrugs his shoulders, and makes another pot of coffee.

On his knees and surrounded by three young employees who hook filmy white shields over their ears to cover their chin hair, Warren begins to dismantle the motor. With greasy parts in both hands, he pushes back through the doors with his elbows and heads for the basement, a spare parts emporium. A quick casual sideways glance and a tight smile tells those in the room near the window waiting to begin their jobs that he's on it.

John says a newer model filler sits in the basement but no one has had time to get it installed. Soon, he says, they will get to it. But today Warren digs up parts where he can find them. In an hour or so, however, after repeated trips to the basement, he realizes a run into neighboring Athens, the county seat, a college town, and a hub for local foods in the state, just 20 minutes away, is going to be necessary. He and Logistics Coordinator Eric Lee head for his old blue Subaru. It's 11:30 A.M.

Despite the used equipment, the recycled building, the simple barn-board arrow at the end of the drive that marks the entrance to the creamery, the young men and women who work long hours there — or perhaps it's because of them — there is one thing absolutely astounding about Warren's risky entrepreneurial venture. It's working.

And in Warren's world, working means more than profit because there isn't much of that yet. He speaks in metaphors when he talks about the business. "We're like a cat hanging on a wall," he snaps when asked about profit. "It feels like we're driving every day in handcuffs," he'll retort when asked about capital. "Snowville is limited in growing right now because we can't get enough capital when we need it. We've gotten virtually no capital investment since we started." But in recent months, private investors are beginning to step up and he's hopeful. Slow Money Ohio, established in January 2012, to help entrepreneurs like Warren facilitated a $50,000 loan between an individual investor and the Creamery, enabling the creamery to add a new milk truck. The Creamery just completed its first year of profit and they're proud of it. A $1 million expansion is in the near future. Already, a portable building has been attached to the plant to expand office space. The newer filler has since been installed. But Warren doesn't linger long over the struggles and the baby steps to profit. For him, Snowville is working because he's employing 24 people, paying them living wages, giving them benefits and doing all of this in Meigs County, a county with the second highest unemployment rate in the state. Working means, one way or the other, Snowville's milk leaves the creamery three times a week and is in grocery stores within two days of packaging. Recyclable paper cartons find their place on the shelves of dairy cases in local and regional stores who otherwise offer mostly highly pasteurized homogenized milk from cows in CAFOs in white plastic half-gallon jugs or organic milk which has usually been ultra pasteurized, itself a part of an industrial organic market. Emails, personal notes, sold out dairy cases, frequent publicity in local, regional, and national media, and moral support from local food advocates affirms an important public success for Warren and Victoria. But working means, most of all to them, that the big subsidized dairy operations haven't yet found a way to shut them down.

Warren earned a dairy technology degree from Ohio State University in 1974. Milk was still good then, he remembers. But changes were happening rapidly in milk handling at a time when dairy production across the nation was consolidating. Three years after he graduated, he was heading processing projects for Safeway's Dairy Division in Oakland, California, the world's largest fluid milk processor with the country's first computer-controlled plant. He was busy designing high-tech facilities and working with federal agencies to make changes in how milk is processed and bottled in a new technology-rich world of food processing. In the ten years he was there, however, he began to see the pitfalls of the new systems. Compromises in quality worried him. At the same time childhood obesity rates began to rise as children's milk consumption declined and 30% fat cheese and cheese-like foods became the principal end products of American's dairy cows, replacing Class 1 fluid milk, Warren said. The problems magnified. When plastic gallon jugs were introduced, for example, light exposure compromised flavor, he said. Complaints about the taste could be greatly reduced by pasteurizing at about ten degrees Fahrenheit higher temperature. This led to a trend known as ultra pasteurizing. The cooked flavor of the higher pasteurized product masked the oxidized flavor the milk takes on because of the plastic jugs. Ultra pasteurizing is actually marketed today as an added value to milk. It isn't.

After a ten-year stint that led to disillusionment with the changes in the way milk was being handled, now spreading like wildfire across the nation, Warren left Safeway. He opened a consulting company and built a successful business doing food process design, leading divisions for Dannon, Land O'Lakes, Daisy Brand (his brother is still the CEO there), and Arla Foods, the largest fluid milk in Europe, among others. But he needed more. After three decades in an industry where he saw plants produce 300,000 gallons of highly pasteurized homogenized milk a day, he was drawn to return to his roots, to the homestead his father Bert had built in southern Ohio. He needed to think about making milk. He wanted his children and all children to grow up with real milk, believing deeply that they deserve good food.

When Warren and Victoria met Bill and Stacy, a friendship began that continues today. Bill and Stacy had become dairy grazers over time and were into full time dairying when they met the Taylors. Ten years ago, they acquired a farm they dubbed the "Brick" because of its high red clay content, their second farm and the farm on which their cows now graze and where the Snowville plant sits. The genetically mixed herd of Jersey, Guernsey, Brown Swiss, among others, are milked morning and night with their milk going directly from the milking parlor to the Snowville processing plant less than 100 yards away. "Our cows have been selected over 20 years to produce a high component milk of butterfat and protein," Stacy said. "In our grass system, cows live longer because they exercise a lot moving from pasture to pasture, they have to be fit," she said. "Because they are fit, they calve easier and have fewer health problems." Stacy and Bill's cows are neither supplemented with Recombinant Bovine Somatotrophin, (rBST), an artificially produced growth hormone injected into cows to increase milk production, nor are they dosed routinely with antibiotics.

In the early years, the couple grew organic vegetables, managed a small beef herd and tended chickens and a few hogs. They couldn't make a living though. Stacy began reading about the potentials of grass-based dairying and they decided to give it a try. It took careful tending and a lot of know how learned over the years to create the lush green pastures that blanket the land there today.

In the early years, their dairy cows were producing milk but they were thin on the still undernourished pastures. "We didn't know how to manage the grass. We were running on no sleep and had no support. We just didn't know anyone else who was doing this. People said we were nuts and wouldn't last six months," she said. Through study, conferences, and lots of informal connections with other farmers who were operating grass-fed dairies across the country, as the grass grew on the Brick, so grew their knowledge. "In order to succeed in the dairy business," Stacy said, "cows must produce large volumes of milk, larger than just what's needed to feed their calves.

As dairy farmers, we have put nutrients back into the soil to produce more grass and be able to grow higher energy grasses high in starch and sugar, the carbohydrates." Although they couldn't grow the optimum grass that could exclusively sustain a dairy cow, the kind that grows in New Zealand, Oregon, and Washington state, for example, they have approximated the quality of that grass by feeding just minimal amounts of grain.

As their pastures improved, production stabilized. The cows were beginning to thrive and subsist on mostly grass. But in order to make a living in dairying then, the couple had no choice but to buy into the conventional business model of dairying, watching their fresh, good, milk from their grass fed cows flow into a truck and be mixed with milk from conventional dairies, then shipped hundreds of miles for high temperature pasteurization and homogenization. "There just weren't any other opportunities then," Stacy said. When Warren and Victoria arrived at Warren's homestead nearby and struck up a friendship, they convinced Bill and Stacy otherwise. Deep inside, Warren knew that milk could be processed and packaged the way it used to be, straight from grass-grazed cows to the cartons. The Same Day Dairy concept took shape.

Warren brought a lifetime of developing business plans and operations to the table. "As American investment in dairy plants declined," he said, "I looked to apply my knowledge to design an efficient small scale on-farm milk bottling plant in my community." He believed from experience and a growing public demand for healthy local food that high value milk with the right marketing and distribution plan could retail for less than the mass-produced ultra pasteurized organic milk that would be an alternative to plastic jug milk. Warren would price his high value Snowville milk somewhere in the middle. He believes premium pasture grazed minimally processed milk can increase per capita consumption if regional markets can be established.

Warren elaborates on his guiding principals. He is keen to support local family farms, like Bill and Stacy's, by providing a higher value outlet for their raw milk than they can receive from large national cooperatives. Milk from the cows on the Brick accounts for most of the milk Snowville processes. When the Dix/Hall cows go dry in the winter, another local grazing farm owned by Chris Hamm, who has put his cows on a different breeding cycle, takes over. Recently three small Amish farms have left the conventional dairy market to follow the grazing model and join Snowville. Like the flagship Dix/Hall and Hamm farms, Snowville takes all the milk they can produce and pays the farmers more than they would receive in the conventional marketplace. "They make more money from us and they know they're doing the right thing," John says. As demand for Snowville milk ramps up, John and Warren are looking for more who will change over to grazing if he assures them of a constant market for their milk.

Warren provides full-time jobs plus opportunities for part-time and interns. Employees like John can progress and find pride in helping to provide healthy local food for their community. "And the payroll of these workers contributes to the local economy and tax base," he says. John and his wife left a teaching job and a lawn care business in Columbus to take up a life on the land where each planned to work half time, giving them time to raise their children and grow their own food. It took them 10 years to become financially stable enough to make the move, but they now own 100 acres near the Creamery. They milk a few goats, raise chickens and work a large garden to grow their own food. John began his part-time work in the dairy barn and was excited when Warren broke ground for the creamery. "I'd get in Warren's ear," John laughed. "When are you ready for me? I would ask him over and over." Now John is the plant manager and works three days a week, the days that Snowville milk is packaged.

They work close margins, meticulously estimating local sales to minimize the removal of unsold milk from the shelves. If milk does remain when they make their next delivery to local stores, they pull the product. Unlike conventional milk, which can remain on the shelf for 30 days or more, Snowville's fresh date is 14 days from packaging. And finally, key to Warren's mission is a pledge to promote pasture grazed dairy farming without the use of hormones or antibiotics, additives now controversial in the industry. Warren resists the organic label—however popular it is in soothing simmering concerns among health conscious Americans about food coming from factory farms. "The astronomical expense of organic feed along with the middleman mark up of large national cooperative distributers and processors drives the costs up," he says. "The local dairy farmer who practices exemplary dairying practices provides an alternative to Certified Organic milk, which is expensive and generally older and more heat treated," he says. "Organic can take the focus off of producing the very finest and freshest milk and makes the goal of producing milk to a rigid organic standard at the lowest possible cost." Until recently, grain fed confinement dairies could be certified organic, belying the trust consumers put in the word that to them means happy cows living out long lives in grassy pastures. Adjustments to organic standards, however, have closed the loophole that permitted this practice and now all ruminant animals must be on pasture during the grazing season.

But Warren is tired of seeing happy cows on milk containers. The majority of dairy cows in this country aren't happy, he said, living short confined lives outside the protection of organic standards in unnatural conditions and producing inferior milk that goes on to be highly pasteurized and homogenized. Nor should we be smiling, he says, urging the public and the producers to look beyond, far beyond even the comfort of organic. "We think all of our local initiatives are making a difference," he said, "but sadly these food successes and all the buzz over them are actually somewhat counterproductive. They prevent people from recognizing the terrible controls that the government's big ag programs and big corporations have over our food system. The irony is that our successes are in fact contributing to our complacency and the sense that we're doing all we need to do," he said. He's restless in this position. "We've got to change the people who go to congress, we have to change the balance of political power by changing our state and local representatives. They are the only ones who can be truly held accountable. Leaders in local communities who see the next step can close the gap."

Ohio is an epicenter for the food movement, Warren will tell you. "The very shape of the state bordering important agricultural neighbors, its rich soils and a long agricultural history lends itself to distribution channels that preserve the integrity of a local food system," he said. With small farms and dairies feeding into rural food hubs that feed into urban hubs, he believes there is real sustainable opportunity to spread local food around the state at significant levels. There is a hunger on both sides of the farmers-market table to be connected, to build relationships with each other, to share in real food. As clusters of young entrepreneurs like Erin, Lee, and Bryn grow beyond farmers markets and CSAs, as organic stays as pure and simple as it is on the Northridge Organic Farm, as the Harrison's livestock business continues to practice and celebrate diversity, and as producers like Snowville and Osage Lane ramp up the dairy side with old-fashioned good, healthy milk, and milk products, he believes the voice for political and social change will be loud and uncompromising. He is cautiously optimistic that broad access and food sovereignty will exist in Ohio and that Ohio can lead the way in the local food movement.

Warren is far more than a dairyman. In his vision for a guarantee of local food, he has built Snowville from the ground up to stand as a model and prototype for future plants in other rural, on the farm, locations. He sees other Snowvilles rising up from grassy pastures to provide "Good Food for All" as demand for his and other local products grows as fast and lush as the grass outside that big picture window.

Sidebar 6

Local Food in a Globalized World

The push for local foods runs counter to what appears to be an inexorable march toward long-distance food trade based on economies of scale and efficiency of food production and processing from a purely cost perspective. Ohio's farmers have focused on the marketing of agricultural products, often to distant locations, since the first settlements in the late 1700s. The fertile lands produced good yields and without local buyers, farmers needed to sell transportable commodities with reasonably high value to bulk ratios. It is no surprise that the earliest goods shipped down the Ohio River through Louisville included salted pork and bacon — a farmer can walk his hogs to market, whiskey — distilling corn really ups its value, tobacco, and of course wheat and corn — both durable grains with high yields. Today we buy Florida oranges, Georgia peaches, Idaho potatoes, Oregon hazelnuts, and just about everything imaginable from California — we take the seemingly endless supply of diverse foods for granted and rarely consider the rise of refrigerated rail and much later truck and air transport that have promoted regional specialization and timely delivery.

Of course food trade today is truly international. U.S. entrepreneurs spearheaded this expansion with the development of the banana trade in the 1890s. This seminal trade was linked to the development of refrigerated shipping, the rise of multinational food conglomerates, and a shift in U.S. foreign policy toward corporate interests. The pace of the international food trade accelerated during the 1970s as the volume of U.S. imports increased four fold. Grain shipments, which once accounted for most of world agricultural trade, now represent less than 30% by value. Imported vegetables and fruits, excluding bananas, accounted for about 14% of U.S. consumption in the late 1990s and these imports continue to rise. Improving technologies including larger and more efficient container ships and computerized GPS tracking of cargo have permitted goods to be transported long distances more efficiently.

The local foods movement, accounting for perhaps 2% of food sales nationally, swims against this tide of globalization. Helping it along may be the warm winds of global climate change because much fossil fuel is consumed and CO_2 emitted in the transportation, refrigeration, and storage of agricultural products. Studies abound attempting to determine which is more efficient, growing warmth-loving crops in favorable tropical and subtropical locales and then shipping them to the affluent mid-latitudes, or extending the growing season locally with heated greenhouses that consume costly fossil fuels. The mode of shipment is often key in these calculations. Boat and rail shipments are very efficient from an energy standpoint, trucks much less so, consuming about 4x the fuel per ton-mile compared to rail, while air transport is far less efficient consuming 30x the energy per ton-mile. Of course these simple ratios hide many associated energy costs linked to shipment transfers and storage. Air transport is used chiefly for perishable, high value, low weight commodities where simple tons per mile calculations are not that relevant. These energy budget/cost studies do often fail to state the obvious: the most energy efficient path is to eat local foods in season.

The argument for local foods extends well beyond energy budgets or simple economic considerations, although the high cost of fossil fuels and global warming are becoming difficult to argue against. Frequently cited benefits of local foods and local food markets include local economic development feedbacks, health and nutrition benefits, impacts on food security, farmland and greenspace preservation, the development of social capital in a community, preservation of cultivar genetic diversity, reduction of the extent of food safety risks, and environmental quality.

Most if not all of these considerations directly or indirectly weigh in on the local push for local foods. *Local* when applied to food lacks a clear definition and depends on regional geography. Perhaps most common is to consider local as food grown within one's county and bordering counties. The Athens County area in southeast Ohio is a regional leader in support for local food. The longstanding year-round Athens Farmers Market is one of Ohio's oldest and busiest. The three-year-old nationally recognized *30-Mile Meal Project*, initially sponsored by the Athens County Convention and Visitors Bureau and now an independent non-profit organization, provides an umbrella network to link over 140 farms, restaurants, and food stores with consumers.

The *30-Mile Meal Project* is presently expanding to other areas including Granville and Licking County. The Licking County Foods Council, a group of farmers, academics, restaurateurs, and others, was selected to expand the food project's mission into central Ohio. As with so many integrated regional projects, the timing of various initiatives is critical. According to Bryn Bird, the demand for local foods is huge, especially when including nearby Columbus, so a first critical step is to network with more local farmers to increase supplies. At the same time the growing market requires significant investments in food handling and storage capabilities. Denison University has provided some start up funds for the group to facilitate branding and networking activities. Hopefully the project's success will compound as distribution networks expand and the local foods movement gains more visibility.

— Tod Frolking

Appendix I

The Language of Local Food

The movement underway to reacquaint the American public with healthy, good tasting food grown by local farmers brings with it a new language of its own. Here are some of the most common definitions that will help you both as a consumer and an advocate.

30-Mile Meal, 50-Mile Meal, 100-Mile Meal: Consuming primarily food grown or produced within a specific mile radius of where the consumer lives. The distance can vary, but generally is limited by the distance of a round-trip drive.

Carbon Footprint: The total amount of greenhouse gases emitted into the atmosphere by a product during its lifetime from raw materials to manufacture to shipping to use and eventually to the waste stream.

Community Supported Agriculture (CSA): A system of direct food sales where consumers "invest" in a farm for the growing season, and in return receive a weekly or monthly payout of fruits and vegetables. Many CSA's also include meats, cheeses, or value added products in addition to fresh crops.

Farmers Market: A direct marketing approach where consumers purchase goods from growers and producers, typically in an outdoor market setting.

Food Miles: The distance food travels from its place of production to the place where it is consumed. On average, food consumed in the U.S. travels 1,500 miles, but by eating locally this distance and its energy use can be greatly reduced.

Food Hub: A central location that connects producers with buyers by offering a suite of production, distribution, and marketing services that allow farmers to concentrate on growing food and consumers to purchase a wide range of local foods in a single, one-stop location. Food hubs can help open up larger volume markets, such as grocery stores, schools, and institutional sites.

Foodshed: A region producing food for a given market. A foodshed can be defined in a variety of ways, but generally includes the land that the food grows on and the routes it must travel before ending up on consumers' tables.

Free-Range: A method of farming or ranching where livestock are allowed to "roam freely," instead of being confined to a feeding stall or cage. The term is most commonly associated with but not limited to poultry. Similar terms include "cage free," "humanely raised," and "pastured livestock."

High Tunnel or **Hoop House:** An unheated poly-covered structure that provides an intermediate level of weather protection and control as compared to field production or heated greenhouses. The term "high tunnel" seems to refer to large structures, "hoop houses" to smaller units. High tunnels are large enough to walk in, work the soil with equipment, and trellis tomatoes; hoop houses may be smaller and lower. In each, supplemental heat can be added to avoid frost damage and fabric crop covers may be added to reduce solar input. In both, the goal is to extend the growing season.

Genetically Modified Organism (GMO): An organism whose genetic material has been altered through genetic engineering. In relation to food and agriculture, this would include plants, seeds, and livestock that have been genetically engineered in a lab to increase yields or pest resistance, or to enhance desired traits. GMOs are a major concern to communities trying to preserve native seeds and/or traditional practices. They differ from traditional plant/animal breeding where desirable traits are selected for through controlled crossbreeding.

Grass-Fed: A diet for ruminant livestock consisting of nothing other than mother's milk, fresh grass and other flowering plants found in pastures, and grass-type hay from birth to slaughter. The livestock must have continuous access to pasture during the growing season.

Locavore: A person who primarily or exclusively eats foods produced within a predetermined radius from his or her home. Locavore was *The New Oxford American Dictionary*'s word of the year in 2007.

Natural: Food products prepared without the use of artificial flavors or coloring, chemical preservatives, or synthetic ingredients and minimally processed in a way that does not fundamentally alter the raw product.

No-Till Farming: A method of farming where the soil is not plowed or turned before being planted. This method reduces soil erosion and fossil fuel consumption while generally increasing soil organic matter content without tilling. This farming method generally requires more extensive pest control, often with heavier applications of pesticides.

Organic: The USDA National Organic Program (NOP) defines organic as follows:

> *Organic food is produced by farmers who emphasize the use of renewable resources and the conservation of soil and water to enhance environmental quality for future generations. Organic meat, poultry, eggs, and dairy products come from animals that are given no antibiotics or growth hormones. Organic food is produced without using most conventional pesticides; fertilizers made with synthetic ingredients or sewage sludge;*

bioengineering; or ionizing radiation. Before a product can be labeled "organic," a Government-approved certifier inspects the farm where the food is grown to make sure the farmer is following all the rules necessary to meet USDA organic standards. Companies that handle or process organic food before it gets to the local supermarket or restaurant must be certified, too.

The USDA has identified three categories for labeling organic products:

- 100% Organic: Made with 100% organic ingredients;
- Organic: Made with at least 95% organic ingredients;
- Made With Organic Ingredients: Made with a minimum of 70% organic ingredients with strict restrictions on the remaining 30%, including no GMOs (genetically modified organisms).

Products with less than 70% organic ingredients may list organically produced ingredients on the side panel of the package, but may not make any organic claims on the front of the package.

Processed Food: This is a tough one. Unless you pull a carrot from the ground and eat it, unwashed, on site, you are probably eating food that has been altered, or processed in some way. Processing, or preserving, is a good thing in general and has allowed the human race to sustain life through seasons in which little or no growth takes place. The act of processing food gets serious and potentially harmful, however, when substances have been altered through biotechnology to barely resemble their original form. Two rules of thumb from author Michael Pollan: If you can't pronounce the ingredients on the label, don't eat it. If the product has more than five ingredients, don't eat it. Nevertheless, here is the legal definition:

The United States Federal Food, Drug and Cosmetic Act, Section 201, Chapter II, (gg) defines processed food as "any food other than a raw agricultural commodity and includes any raw agricultural commodity that has been subject to processing, such as canning, cooking, freezing, dehydration, or milling." This definition establishes parameters for the Food and Drug Administration, or FDA, to regulate quality and safety in the food processing industry.

Real Food: As used in this new food movement, this term has been coined to encompass many aspects of production. **Good** — Fresh, nutritious and flavorful. **Clean** — Free of toxic chemicals and preservatives. **Fair** — Farmers realize a fair price for their products and earn a living wage.

Slow Food: An international movement to preserve traditional and regional foods started as an organization in Italy in 1986 in response to the intrusion of fast food. Now with 100,000 members in 150 countries. Five chapters are in Ohio.

Sustainable Agriculture: An integrated farm system that satisfies human food and fiber needs, enhances environmental quality, makes the most efficient use of resources and integrates natural biological cycles and controls, sustains the economic viability of farm operations, and enhances the quality of life for farmers, animals and society as a whole.

Value-Added Product: A raw agricultural product that has been modified or enhanced to have a higher market value and/or a longer shelf life. Some examples include herbs made into spices, fruits made into pies or jams, meats made into jerky, and tomatoes, peppers, and onions made into salsa.

Appendix II

Supporting Ohio's Local Food Systems

These organizations can provide further information on the issues and content of the new local food movement in Ohio.

The Appalachian Center for Economic Networks

The mission of the Appalachian Center for Economic Networks (ACEnet) is to build networks, support innovation, and facilitate collaboration with Appalachian Ohio's businesses to create a strong, sustainable regional economy.
www.acenetworks.org

Edible Columbus

Edible Columbus is an independently owned, community-based publication devoted to connecting you to your local food community. The magazine focuses on local, sustainable food sources and the people who work the land. Featured regularly to empower a true local food system are farmers, distributors, local artisans, entrepreneurs, and leaders. Regional issues of *Edible* magazines print in Cincinnati and Cleveland as well.
www.ediblecolumbus.com

The Going Green Store

"A general store for the modern world." This Granville eco-general store offers a local foods section with fresh produce; a refrigerated area for milk, eggs, and meat; and dry goods, all from local producers. Their 50-Mile Food & Friends project aims to support the local economy, support good health, and seek out environmentally and socially sustainable products.
www.thegoinggreenstore.com

Green Bean Delivery

Green Bean Delivery is a privately held organization located in Columbus, Cleveland, and Cincinnati, and with centers in Indiana and Kentucky, to help farmers move product directly to consumers via a home or workplace delivery service as well as business and institutional delivery of local products.

www.greenbeandelivery.com

The Greener Grocer

The Greener Grocer market stand located within the North Market in Columbus offers sustainably grown food from local farms. It champions "buy local" efforts to build a strong community and support the local foodshed. Other small grocery stores around Ohio are beginning to feature locally grown and produced foods along this model.

www.thegreenergrocer.com

Local Matters

Local Matters is a non-profit organization in central Ohio committed to transforming the food system to one less vulnerable to fluctuations in the economy or among policy makers, to connect people to their food and make the region more resilient and able to survive a catastrophic event or economic downturn. A prosperous food system ensures fair prices to both producers and consumers, accounts for the true cost of creating healthy soil and nutrition, and keeps wealth within the community by supporting local vendors. It works toward a just system and recognizes that a delicious food system creates joy and community around the table.

www.local-matters.org

Northeast Ohio Food Web

Northeast Ohio Food Web has emerged in the last five years as a national leader in the development of sustainable local food systems capitalizing on innovative public-private partnerships. With funding from the Cleveland Foundation, a process to develop a strategic business plan is being written to take local food markets to scale. The major goal of the Northeast Ohio Local Food Assessment Plan is to create a significant economic development strategy for the region based on the production, processing, and distribution of local food.

www.neofoodweb.org

Ohio Ecological Food & Farm Association

The Ohio Ecological Food & Farm Association (OEFFA) was founded in 1979 and is a grassroots coalition of farmers, backyard gardeners, consumers, retailers, educators, researchers, and others who share a desire to build a healthy food system that brings prosperity to family farmers, helps preserve farmland, offers food security for all Ohioans, and creates economic opportunities for our rural communities. OEFFA serves as the state's largest certification organization for the National Organic Association.

www.oeffa.org

Ohio Farmers Union

The Ohio Farmers Union pursues public policy that supports the family farmer and consumers. The organization supports and advocates on behalf of legislation that recognizes the unique market realities of family farmers. The OFU believes that consumers benefit from robust local farming economies that support locally grown and produced food and fiber.

www.ohfarmersunion.org

Ohio Produce Growers & Marketers Association

The Ohio Produce Growers & Marketers Association is an organization whose goal is to produce exceptional quality crops, for consumers and processors, utilizing environmentally friendly practices. OPGMA provides educational opportunities to businesses, families, and employees associated with the production and marketing of Ohio's fresh produce.

www.opgma.org

Slow Food Columbus

Slow Food Columbus as part of Slow Food USA and the founding organization Slow Food International works towards a more sustainable food system by establishing and strengthening the foundations of pleasurable eating, including developing an appreciation for food quality, defending biodiversity, and fostering pleasure in eating meals with others.

www.slowfoodcolumbus.org

Slow Money Columbus

Established in 2009, the non-profit organization Slow Money Columbus formed to steer significant sources of capital to small food enterprises, appropriate-scale organic farming, and local food systems. The group works to catalyze an emerging "nurture capital" industry. There are chapters in Columbus, Cleveland, and Cincinnati.

www.slowmoneyohio.org

Sources

Print Sources

Brown, Ralph H. 1948. *Historical Geography of the United States*. New York, NY: Harcourt Brace.

Feenstra, Gail. 2002. "Creating space for sustainable food systems: Lessons from the field." *Agriculture and Human Values* 19(2): 99–106.

Hart, John Fraser. 1972. "The Middle West" *Annals of the Association of American Geographers* 62(2): 258–282.

Kingsolver, Barbara. 2007. *Animal, Vegetable, Miracle: A Year of Food Life*. New York, NY: Harper Collins.

Lal, Rattan. 2007. "Carbon management in agricultural soils." *Mitigation and Adaption Strategies for Global Change* 12(2): 303–322.

Parkinson, Robert J., Michael L. Wiggington, and Paul C. Jenny. 1992. *Soil Survey of Licking County, Ohio*. Washington, DC: United States Department of Agriculture, Soil Conservation Service.

Pollan, Michael. 2006. *The Omnivore's Dilemma: A Natural History of Four Meals*. New York, NY: The Penguin Press.

Pollan, Michael. 2009. *Food Rules*. New York, NY: The Penguin Press.

Ruddiman, William. 2005. *Plows, Plagues and Petroleum: How Humans Took Control of Climate*. Princeton, NJ: Princeton University Press.

Taylor, John, Matina Madrick, and Sam Collin. 2005. *Trading Places: The Local Economic Impact of Street Produce and Farmers' Markets.* London, UK: Report by The New Economics Foundation for the London Development Agency.

Digital Sources

"Children's Life Expectancy being Cut Short by Obesity," *The New York Times*, March 17, 2005.
www.nytimes.com/2005/03/17/health/17obese.html

Coalition for Food Sovereignty. *www.vermontfoodsovereignty.net*

Dairy Goats: A National Information Center for Value-Added Agriculture. Agricultural Marketing Resource Center. *www.agmrc.org*

Environmental Working Group, 2011 Farm Subsidy Database. *www.farm.ewg.org*

Food and Agriculture Organization of the United Nations, FAOSTAT, comprehensive past and present data on hunger, food and agriculture for 245 countries.
http://faostat3.fao.org/home/index.html

"Health and Economic Burden of Projected Obesity Trends in the USA and the UK." The Lancet. August 27, 2011. *www.thelancet.com*

Heritage Turkey Foundation. *www.heritageturkeyfoundation.org*

Licking County Planning Commission, Agriculture for Tomorrow. *http://www.lcounty.com/Planning/Agriculture/default.aspx*

Meter, Ken. Ohio's Food Systems — Farms at the Heart of it All. Crossroads Resource Center. March 2011.
www.crcworks.org/ohfood.pdf

National Young Farmers Coalition, Citizen Action Program, Open Space Institute, Inc. *www.youngfarmers.org*

Ohio Department of Natural Resources, Ohio Geological Survey, Surficial Geology, page with maps of glacial deposits and Ohio topography among others. *http://www.dnr.state.oh.us/OhioGeologicalSurvey/SurficialGeology/tabid/23586/Default.aspx*

Ohio Ecological Food and Farm Association (OEFFA). *www.oeffa.org/certification.php/*

Taylor, Nicholas. Back from the Brink, Edible East Bay, Edible Communities Publications. Fall/Winter 2009. *www.ediblecommunities.com*

U.S. Belted Galloway Society. *www.beltie.org*

U.S. Department of Agriculture, 2002 Census of Agriculture. *http://www.agcensus.usda.gov/Publications/2002/Volume 1, Chapter 1 State Level/Ohio/*

U.S. Department of Agriculture, Agricultural Marketing Service, Farmers Markets and Local Food Marketing. *http://www.ams.usda.gov/AMSv1.0/FARMERSMARKETS*

U.S. Department of Agriculture, Agricultural Marketing Service, Farmers Market Directory. *http://search.ams.usda.gov/farmersmarkets/*

U.S. Department of Agriculture, Economic Research Service, current data on agricultural production in Ohio. *http://www.ers.usda.gov/data-products/state-fact-sheets.aspx*

U.S. Department of Agriculture, National Organic Program. *http://www.ams.usda.gov/AMSv1.0/nop*

U.S. Department of Agriculture, Natural Resources Conservation Service, Soil Survey Manual, Chapter 3 – Examination and Description of Soils. *http://soils.usda.gov/technical/manual/contents/chapter3.html*

U.S. Department of Energy, (2012) Transportation Energy Data Book, Edition 31. *http://cta.ornl.gov/data/download31.shtml*

U.S. Environmental Protection Agency, Pesticide Market Estimates, 2006–2007. *www.epa.gov/opp00001/pestsales/.../table_of_contents 2007.htm*

Index